LEVI INGLEDUE

LEGENDS AND LEGACIES

Levi Ingledue – Legends and Legacies

Manufactured in the United States of America.

Published by
AABMC Publications, LLC
P.O. Box 843
Yellow Springs, OH 45387
United States

Hunnibell, Mark L
        Levi Ingledue – Legends and Legacies
        Library of Congress Control Number: 2023938191
        ISBN (Paperback): 978-1-7346451-3-2

Cover design by Mark Hunnibell
Illustrations by Rachel Reddy
Other maps and charts by Mark Hunnibell

FOREWORD

I am Mark Leslie Hunnibell, husband to Laura Hunnibell, born Laura Sue Ingledue. We have been married for over 30 years. During that time, I met many members of her extended family. By the 1990s, I had become engaged in researching my family's genealogy. Laura saw my passion and skill in this area and asked if I could help solve a longstanding mystery in her family.

It seems that no one living knew the origins of her 2nd Great Grandfather, Levi Ingledue. One of his grandsons had asked Levi back in the 1920s. Levi said he'd been "hatched out on a stump in the woods." For the young boy, the answer made no sense at all. But even he got the idea it was something Levi didn't want to discuss, so he just didn't.

My research has revealed why he was so cautious. He probably believed that most people did not need to know, even if he, at some point, had confided the truth to at least some of his children.

This book is the product of a substantial effort to research the facts and history of Levi's ancestors going back to the 17th Century in County York and Durham in North East England. Because there is so much information and documentation that isn't in this book, additional information is available on a unique Ingledue family website set up just for that purpose:

https://www.INGLEDUE.net

If any Ingledues (or relations) read this book and the materials on the website and would like to contribute additional information or make corrections or comments, please use the form on the website or send an email to laura@ingledue. net, and we will follow up.

For my Laura Sue,

Mark Hunnibell
Yellow Springs, Ohio

DEDICATION

This book is dedicated to my wife, born Laura Sue Ingledue. Her gentle prodding, encouragement, and editorial help assisted me in solving and documenting a long-standing mystery in her family, telling the story in a compassionate manner that is intended to be informative, engaging, and entertaining for readers of all ages.

This book is my gift to Laura
and the rest of the Family Ingledue.

Mark Leslie Hunnibell

CONTENTS

FRONT MATTER: . . . . i-xvi

CHAPTER 1: Happy Birthday 1-12
CHAPTER 2: Coming to America. 13-30
CHAPTER 3: Getting Started 31-44
CHAPTER 4: More Ingledue Migration 45-54
CHAPTER 5: The Next Generation 55-66
CHAPTER 6: West to Ohio 67-80
CHAPTER 7: Jacob Cook and Elizabeth Ingledue 81-88
CHAPTER 8: Meeting Judith Parrott. 89-96
CHAPTER 9: Lewis Rue Ingledue and His Son Martin . 97-104
CHAPTER 10: Judith Emily Parrott's Heritage 105-126
CHAPTER 11: The Wedding of Levi Ingledue and Judith . . . . .
    Emily Parrott. 127-138
CHAPTER 12: Levi's Growing Family. 139-154
CHAPTER 13: Conclusion 155-158

APPENDIX

APPENDIX A: Previous Ingledue Genealogy. . . . . . . A-1 - A-12
APPENDIX B: DNA Analysis . . . . B-1 - B-8
APPENDIX C: Areas Requiring Further Study. . . . . . . C-1 - C-4
APPENDIX D: Historic and Current Prevalence of Ingledews .
    in Yorkshire . . . . D-1 - D-4
BIBLIOGRAPHY. . . . . Bib-1 - Bib-8
ACKNOWLEDGEMENTS. Ack-1 - Ack-2
ABOUT THE AUTHOR. . . . . Author-1 - Author-3

ILLUSTRATIONS, PHOTOGRAPHS, MAPS, & GENEALOGY TREES

FRONTISPIECE: Levi Ingledue iv

FIGURE 1: Levi's 80th Birthday Dinner, Harrod, Ohio xvi
Illustration by Rachel Reddy

FIGURE 2: Levi's 80th Birthday Cake 3
Illustration by Rachel Reddy

FIGURE 3: Ingledew Origins in Northeast England 15

FIGURE 4: William Ingledew, wives, and children 21

FIGURE 5: Blackstone and Margaret Ingledew arrive in
Philadelphia in 1725 27
Illustration by Rachel Reddy

FIGURE 6: Bank Meeting House, Front St, Philadelphia 33
Artist Unknown (Public Domain)

FIGURE 7: Map of Philadelphia in 1776 with inset of
locations for Parrock and Ingledue 34-35

FIGURE 8: Blackstone Life Spans 37

FIGURE 9: Early 18th Century Blackstone Ingledew, wives, . . .
and children 39

FIGURE 10: Ingledue Migration to Goose Creek . . . .
Monthly Meeting, Loudoun County, Virginia 47

FIGURE 11: Children of Blackstone Ingledue and . . . .
their spouses 51

FIGURE 12: Children of Blackstone Ingledue II and . . . .
Ann Rue and their spouses 56-57

FIGURE 13: Ingledue Migration to Goose Creek . . . .
Monthly Meeting, Bedford County, Virginia 59

FIGURE 14: Ingledue Migrations to Ohio 69

FIGURE 15: Patterson Ingledue Migration to Ohio
County, West Virginia. 69

FIGURE 16: Northeast Townships in Columbiana . . . .
County, Ohio 71

FIGURE 17: William Ingledue & Magdalen Erwin . . . .
and children. 75

FIGURE 18: Duchouquet, Union, and Wayne Townships . . . .
in Allen/Auglaize Counties, Ohio 78-79

FIGURE 19: Lewis Rue Ingledue and Nancy Erwin . . . .
and children 99

FIGURE 20: Lewis Rue Ingledue Migration to Marshall . . . . . .
County, Iowa 99

FIGURE 21: Lineage from Blackstone Ingledue II to . . . .
Martin Ingledue and Levi Ingledue 101

FIGURE 22: Origins of Frederick Parrett in Europe 107

FIGURE 23: Parrott Migration to Shenandoah County, ...
Virginia 109

FIGURE 24: Frederick Parrett and Barbara Edwards and . . . . .
children 112-113

FIGURE 25: Two Generations of Descendants from John . . . . .
Preston Parrett and Catherina Meyers and one . . . .
generation from Louise "Lucy" Bean 114-115

FIGURE 26: Parrott Migration to Parrottsville, Tennessee . 117

FIGURE 27: Parrott Migration into Ohio 119

FIGURE 28: "Blackbearded John" Parrott children with Mary.
Nancy Copeland and Rachel Kirkpatrick Stevenson . . . .
Whitcomb 125

FIGURE 29: Judith Emily Parrott and Levi Ingledue on . . . . . .
their wedding day, 30 Oct 1862 129
Illustration by Rachel Reddy

FIGURE 30: "Blackbearded John" Parrott and Rachel . . . .
Kirkpatrick Stevenson Whitcomb, 30 Oct 1862 131

FIGURE 31: Four generations of Levi Ingledue's . . . .
descendants as of his 80th birthday 140-141

FIGURE 32: Levi Ingledue and his crew with Ox-drawn . . . . .
D. June Steam Engine, ca. 1883 141
Illustration by Rachel Reddy

FIGURE 33: Levi Ingledue and Daughter Amy with D. June . .
Traction Engine, ca. 1889 143

FIGURE 34: The children of Levi Ingledue, ca. 1898 145

FIGURE 35: Levi and his children, ca. 1903 149

FIGURE 36: Levi and his daughters, 1912 151

FIGURE 37: A.C. Dawson, ca. 1885 . . . . Appendix A - 11

FIGURE 38: DNA Test Group and Matches . . . Appendix B - 7

BACK COVER: James Arthur Ingledue and granddaughter,
Shirley Ann Ingledue

All maps, tables, and genealogical trees created by Mark Hunnibell.

All photographs in this book have been digitally retouched.

Figure 1: Levi's 80th Birthday Dinner, Harrod, Ohio

CHAPTER 1:
HAPPY BIRTHDAY

Levi looked down at the long table and could see the excited faces of everyone seated and milling around outside on an unusually warm October 11, 1921. His daughter Sadie[1] and her husband, George Krouskop, were hosting Levi's 80th birthday party at their house in the country between Harrod Village and Westminster in Auglaize Township in Allen County, Ohio.[2] Family and friends had come from miles around to celebrate this milestone.

An industrious man his whole life, he had only recently stopped actively working and was now living in George and

---

1   Sadie's name given at birth was Sarah Catherine Ingledue, but she was known to family as Sadie.

2   The street address for this home is now 2120 Hullibarger Rd, Harrod, OH 45850. The house was on an 8-acre lot across the road from their barn and over 80 acres of farmland.

Sadie's house, so he only had to walk off the porch to join the festivities. His 11 children, their spouses, and most of his 30 grandchildren were there. Two of Martin Ingledue's[3] children also came: Inez Ingledue Fess, then 53 years old, lived nearby in Lima, Ohio, but her younger brother Charlie Ingledue, then 49 years old, also came while visiting from California. Their father, Martin, had passed away 11 years earlier, in 1910. Martin had lived in Allen County for most of his adulthood and was a good friend to Levi. Levi's children often referred to him as "Uncle Mart," perhaps not knowing his true relationship with Levi. But Levi had known Martin, who was four years older than Levi, for many years and knew they were second cousins. Thus, Martin was not an uncle to any of Levi's children.

After their meal, Levi excused himself and retired to his favorite rocking chair. His daughter Sadie had moved the chair off the porch onto the grass lawn. She placed a small table next to Levi. Then she brought out a traditional birthday cake with 80 candles. Somehow, Sadie was able to get most of the candles lit despite the light breeze. A cake was a rare luxury for a hard-working family like the Ingledues. But there it was, and they were all going to have some! While the family gathered around and sang "Happy Birthday," the children ran around with expectant eagerness, each knowing they would soon be getting a real treat: a piece of birthday cake!

---

3   Martin Ingledue was the son of Lewis Rue Ingledue, who had migrated west from Columbiana County in Ohio to Marshall County in Iowa in the 1860s, depositing family members along the way.

Figure 2: Levi's 80th Birthday Cake

After everyone had received their cake, Levi quietly stood up and walked over to the three-rail fence that separated the yard from the field where horses and cows grazed. He leaned lightly on the top rail and looked to the horizon, taking in the view; it was all farmland as far as his eyes could see.

He began reflecting on his life. It had been one of extraordinary success, but not without significant challenges. Levi was proudest of his family. He knew well the hard work it took to raise 11 children to adulthood and see them have their own children. Many of those grandchildren were now playing and running around the yard behind him.

With a faraway look in his eyes, he gazed into the field, recalling a significant event from his childhood. He and his mother were returning home after walking a mile to the market in Waynesfield. Levi remembered an event he knew had taken place just six or seven miles south of where he was now standing.

It was a brisk day in April 1849. Levi and his mother had walked to the market in town. Levi was not even eight years old, but he was proud to be able to help his mother, who he could see would soon be having a fourth child. His mother asked if they could stop and rest for a few minutes. They paused on a small hill by the roadside under a lone apple tree. From there, they could see far into the distance; miles of gently rolling landscape dotted with fields. They sat in silence and enjoyed the sun's warmth, listening to the birds singing about how happy they were that winter was over. After a few minutes of contemplation, his mother said, "Levi, I need to tell you a special story."

Levi had always liked listening to his mother's stories with his two brothers, who – in truth – were too young to appreciate them, so he sat up and listened attentively, knowing he could listen without distraction.

Mama started the story with a friendly – but stern – warning, "Now Levi, I want to tell you something important that I want you never to forget, but also never to trust anyone else to hear. This story will be your secret for as long you shall live."

"But why does it have to be a secret?" Levi asked.

"It may be hard to understand that right now, but perhaps after I tell you the story, you'll understand. People can sometimes be cruel to you because of things that are not your fault." Although it made perfect sense to his mother, it seemed like gibberish to Levi, who replied, "Mama, I don't understand."

Mama calmly explained, "I think you'll need to live more of your life to understand what I mean, but will you promise to me right now that you'll remember this day for the rest of your life and remember this story in your most secret hiding place?"

Levi had always trusted his mother. He could sense the sincerity and seriousness of her tone, even though it was confusing, so he made the promise.

Now, over 70 years later, with a faraway look, Levi remembered that day and saw the wisdom of the pledge his mother had asked of him. He had listened attentively to the story. He came to believe that people would unfairly judge him or his mother if they heard the story, so he had done his best to keep the promise since then.

Before his mother even began telling the story, Levi knew he had been born on October 11, 1841, and that his mother, Rebecca Ingledue, had married Joseph Dawson a month later. Joseph was 59 years old when they married and his marriage to Rebecca had begun as something of a trade. Joseph's first wife, Elizabeth, had died two years earlier, leaving Joseph at home with the last of their sons, aged 12, 13, 16, and 19. So Joseph married Rebecca to help finish raising his sons, and, in exchange, he provided her with a safe home in which she could protect and care for young Levi.

However, the marriage turned out to be more than one of convenience because Rebecca soon gave Joseph two more sons, Alvin (or "AC" as he came to be known) in 1844, and

Milton in 1846. By April 1849, Rebecca was 41 years old and pregnant again. It could be that she knew the risks of having a baby so late in life and thought this lovely spring day in April was an excellent opportunity to tell the whole story to Levi in private.

Now that she had Levi's attention and solemn promise, Rebecca began.

"AC and Milt are known as 'half-brothers' because you don't have the same father. Papa Dawson isn't your father, but AC and Milt are also my sons. When you get older, you'll understand that most people who have babies are married. Although God sanctions marriage between a man and a woman to be recognized within the community to have children, it's possible to have children without marriage." After a long pause, in a soft voice – almost a whisper – she said, "I wasn't married to your father."

Levi followed what his mother said, but this didn't seem like much of a secret. Even though he thought of AC and Milt as his brothers, he knew they were his "half-brothers." If they'd been his full brothers, Papa Dawson would have been his father, and he would have been named Levi Dawson. Also, while AC and Milt called their father "Papa," Levi had always called him "Papa Dawson." So Levi already knew all this! He challenged his mother, "But that's no secret!"

Rebecca answered solemnly, "Levi, do you remember not long ago when you asked me who your father was?"

"Yes. I remember. You said that boys didn't need to have a father, that a mother was enough."

Rebecca said, "While it's true that you don't always need a father in a home, it's also true that a man is needed to make a baby with a woman, even if the man and woman are only together for a short time and the man does not stay."

Levi caught on but started peppering his mother with questions, each becoming even more serious, "So my father went away? Why did he go away? Did he not love me like you? Is this all my fault?"

Rebecca said, "If the man who made you had been married to me, some of those would be questions to be answered, but it's never your fault. If anyone is to blame, it's me."

Levi could not imagine his mother had done anything wrong, so he immediately thought that some man had done something terrible.

Rebecca could see the anger welling in Levi's face and tried to reassure him, "The man brought you to me so I could bring you into this world, love you, and raise you. That's a good thing. That's the only thing that matters. That's why I told you that boys didn't need to have a father, that a mother was enough."

Rebecca continued, saying, "I know that you told me you would keep this story a secret, but the man lives nearby, and it would upset some people if they learned that you were his son. I think it's best not to risk disturbing the peace. But I also think you deserve to know when you're grown up. It's not easy to understand your place in the world if you don't know the man and woman who brought you into it. After your 18th birthday, I'll tell you if you still want to know. By then, I think you'll understand how important it's to continue to keep this a secret. You might even decide it's just not that important."

When Levi asked his mother if it was a secret that Rebecca and Joseph were married and that AC and Milton were his half-brothers, she answered quickly, "Of course, that's not a secret! Everyone knows all that."

Levi asked for confirmation that the only secret was who his father was and that he could never reveal it even after he turned 18. Rebecca said, "Yes. Do you have any other questions?"

Levi paused, then asked, "Mama, why do some fathers not stay home with their boys?"

Rebecca thought carefully about how to answer in a way her young son would understand. She told Levi that, "Not all fathers can stay, so their mothers have to love their boys twice as much. But God is our father in heaven, and He will always love you as his own."

Then Rebecca lowered her head and quietly added, "I know who my mother was, but I never knew my father. So I know you can grow up big and strong without a father. But that's a story for another day."

Levi said, "No, Mama, tell me that story now! Tell me THAT story."

Rebecca leaned back, let out a big sigh, and pondered Levi's request. It seemed to her like young Levi was looking for reassurance. So Rebecca and Levi sat under that apple tree for many more hours while Rebecca told Levi about his family's history. She began with the most distant ancestor she knew much about, Blackstone Ingledue.

"Blackstone was born over 150 years ago in England. His parents were good Quakers, but they died, leaving him an orphan when he was less than three years old. In early 1725, when Blackstone was 29 years old, he made the dangerous Atlantic Ocean voyage to Philadelphia accompanied by his bride, Margaret, who would have a baby soon. Blackstone became the grand patriarch of a vast family of Ingledue descendants, including you and me!"

"Blackstone! Was he a pirate?" Levi exclaimed, jumping up and waving an imaginary sword in the air.

"No, Levi," Rebecca laughed gently, "he wasn't a pirate! Now sit down and listen."

She continued, "You've done very well learning to read and write, especially your name. There is a funny story about our last name, Ingledue. I showed you how to spell it with a D-U-E at the end of it, remember?"

Levi sat up, drew the letters in the air, and proudly said, "D-U-E."

"But it wasn't always like that," she continued. "Back in England, they spelled it with a D-E-W at the end. But over the last 150 years in America, most people changed it to D-U-E. Sometimes people still spell it with D-E-W or even D-O-O. These differences are mostly because some people don't read or write very well, a skill I've told you many times is important. It's why you need to pay attention to your studies."

Levi nodded his understanding, leaned forward into the soft grass, and, without saying a word, begged his mother to continue.

CHAPTER 2:
COMING TO AMERICA

Levi listened intently as his mother began telling the tale of William Ingledew, explaining that William was Levi's third great-grandfather. "Grandpa William," she said, "was born almost 200 years ago in old England."[4] She told Levi that the Ingledews were a prosperous family of ocean-going sailors or mariners. They were also some of the earliest members of the Society of Friends, called the Quakers. "Grandpa William owned several ships, some that could cross the ocean with names like *Friends' Adventure*."[5]

---

4   Quaker records suggest William Ingledew was born in 1656 in Seamer-in-Cleveland, North Riding, Yorkshire.

5   William Ingledew's 6 Aug 1698 will identifies a ship named *Friends' Adventure* as being bequeathed to his daughter. This vessel might not be the same *Friends' Adventure* that was part of William Penn's "fleet" of 22 ships loaded with Quakers that began arriving in Philadelphia in 1682 (with Thomas Wall as Master sailing from Liverpool). Also, several

Was _he_ a pirate?" Levi exclaimed, again jumping up and waving his imaginary sword.

"No, dear Levi, Grandpa William was a hard-working businessman who was a master and mariner on big ships that sailed all over the world from ports in Stockton-on-Tees, Sunderland, and South Shields in northeast England."

Levi flooded his mother with more questions: "What's a Quaker?" "What's a mariner?" "What part of Ohio is England in?" "Where's the ocean?" Rebecca knew the answers would help Levi, so she patiently answered them.

Rebecca explained Quakers in the simplest way she could, reflecting her general knowledge of the faith but using words and ideas she hoped Levi would grasp. She explained to Levi that outsiders began using the word "Quakers" to identify the members of a new religious faith, the Society of Friends, formed in the mid-1600s in England. The Church of England didn't like Quakers because they held "non-conforming" views about how to be good Christians.

She told Levi, "Quakers hold the conviction that there is a connection to God within every person. They believe that love is at the heart of existence. They believe that all human beings are unique and equal; therefore, every person matters, even people we may not like very much."

---

decades after William Ingledew died, a ship named _Friends' Adventure_ was being used on trans-Atlantic routes from England to Philadelphia. Even though the name seems conspicuous, it is possible these are three different vessels that share a name only by coincidence.

Figure 3: Ingledew Origins in Northeast England

Rebecca explained that Quakers kept detailed records about their members and lived by strict community rules. One rule was that a Quaker could only marry another Quaker. Even then, the Quaker Meeting would have to approve of the marriage. She added that if a Quaker disobeyed the rules, the Society often disowned them.

Levi did not understand the meaning or relevance of any of this, but he quickly recalled what she had just said about Quaker views regarding God. Levi asked, "Do Quakers believe that I have part of God in me and that God is not just my father in heaven?"

Rebecca marveled at how her young son remembered what she had said an hour ago and connected it to her explanation about Quakers and God. She paused and then said, "I suppose so, yes. Even though we're not Quakers, it's good to believe there is a part of God in you."

Levi asked, "Where are their churches?"

"They don't have churches." Rebecca explained, "Quakers meet in small groups called Meetings, often at the home of one of the members. But some have what they call Meeting Houses where they gather, instead of churches."

Levi said, "I've never seen one. Are there any of them around here?"

"There were quite a few where I used to live, in Columbiana County about 200 miles away, but there are no Quaker Meetings near here," Rebecca said, "but let me tell you the rest of the beginning of the story about 'Grandpa William.'"

Levi paused, gave it some thought, and then nodded for his mother to continue the story.

Rebecca continued, "Grandpa William Ingledew married Margaret Marshall in 1675 when he was 19 years old and Margaret was 22.[6] They were both Quakers and received permission from the Meeting to be married. Their first baby, Anna, died the same year she was born in 1678, but Caleb came along four years later.[7] William also became qualified as a Master and Mariner. That means he was qualified to work as a captain on gigantic ships that sailed the ocean, with colorful names such as *Friend's Adventure*.[8] But Margaret died when Caleb was only eight years old, the same age you're close to right now. Grandpa William could see Caleb was sorrowful and missed his mother, so he received permission to marry another Quaker woman, Alice Blackstone.[9] Grandpa William and Alice had two more

6   William Ingledew married Margery Marshall on 23 Nov 1675. Some records use "Margery Martial" as her name, but these are likely due to the literacy of scribes who often wrote the names as they heard them.

7   Caleb was born on 11 Oct 1682.

8   This ship, *Friends' Adventure*, and several other ships are identified by name in William's 6 Aug 1698 will as being owned outright or in partnership with others. The will stated that these assets should be sold with proceeds reserved for use by his daughter Elizabeth.

9   William Ingledew and Alice Blackstone were married on 13 Jul 1690.

babies, Elizabeth and Blackstone, in 1693[10] and 1696.[11] But when Blackstone was only a year old, his mother, Alice, died.[12] Grandpa William had previously hired Mary Hunter, a Quaker, to come to live in his home and care for his three children as a governess and tutor. In his will, Grandpa William provided for Mary to continue in those roles after he died."

---

10   Elizabeth Ingledew was born on 8 Oct 1893.

11   Blackstone Ingledew was born on 1 Feb 1695/96. This "dual year" style of date is used in this book to reflect how dates were reflected using the Julian calendar in use by countries like England but changed to the modern, Gregorian, calendar in 1752. The Quakers adapted to this new calendar but did not like using the named months or even the names for days of the week. The Quakers would refer to dates numerically, such as "the 15th day of the 9th month in 1722," but sometimes included clarifying text like "the 15th day of the 9th month called November in 1722." The "Old Style" Julian calendar began each year on March 25th. The result was that a date like 24 Mar 1730, was followed by 25 Mar 1731 (Quakers referred to January as the 11th month and February as the 12th month. It is unclear how officials referred to the month number for a date in March prior to the new year.) The effect of these changes is that the modern convention is to reflect such dates as "dual year" as shown above for Blackstone's birth date of 1 Feb 1695/96 (which reflects that, using today's calendar, he was born on 1 Feb 1696, but when he was born, they just called it 1 Feb 1695, or the "first day of the 12th month anno 1695"). Also, although it is a fact unrelated to this "dual year" issue, a minor discrepancy exists in that some Quaker records reflect Blackstone's date of birth as being 31 Jan 1695/96.

12   On 1 Feb 1696/97, Alice Blackstone Ingledew died at 32, coincidentally on the first anniversary of her son Blackstone's birth, and was interred at the Friends Burying Ground in Cullercoats, North Shields, Northumberland, England. This cemetery has been moved over the years (for roads, etc.). There is no available list of the locations of those buried there or precisely where they have been relocated. Documentation supporting Alice's burial at the Friends Burying Ground in Cullercoats comes from Quaker Meeting minutes.

Levi interrupted, "Is that like what Joseph did when Lewis, Newton, and Jonathan's mother died? Did he hire you to come and take care of his house?"

Rebecca was again amazed at Levi's ability to compare the story with his circumstance. "Yes, it's very similar, but Grandpa William didn't marry Mary Hunter, and they didn't have any children together."

Levi asked, "What happened next?"

Rebecca lowered her voice and solemnly said, "Grandpa William died[13] only a year and a half after Alice died. His three children were now true orphans. Caleb was almost a man at age 15, but Elizabeth was only four years old, and Blackstone wasn't quite two years old."

Levi again compared his life to the lives of his ancestors, "Does that means that when Grandpa William died, Blackstone was younger than my little brother Milton is today?"

Rebecca was getting used to Levi's comparative analysis by now, so she just said, "Yes. It was an unfortunate time for

---

13   William Ingledew died 23 August, 1698, in South Shields, Durham, England.

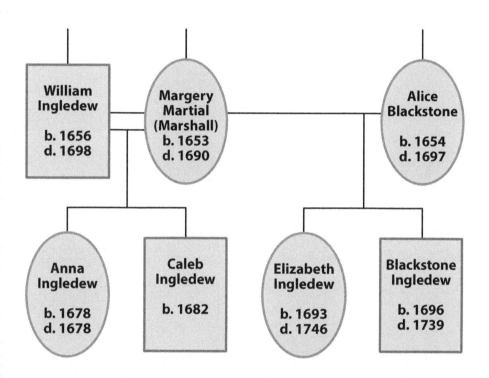

Figure 4: William Ingledew (1656-1698),
wives, and children

the Ingledew children. All three had lost their parents in less than ten years." She paused because she saw Levi looking into the distance as if to internalize and reflect on this and how it might be for himself in similar circumstances.

When she saw Levi was ready, she continued. "When Grandpa William died, he owned many things. He signed a legal document called a will to tell people what he wanted them to do with his property after he died."

"In his will," Rebecca said, "Grandpa William left money for Mary Hunter to pay any debts due when he died and to allow her to continue to raise his children until they were grown. He left his family's land in Newby in northern Yorkshire to his firstborn son, Caleb. He left ships and other valuable things to Elizabeth for when she got older. But then he left only five shillings to little Blackstone."

"What's a shilling?" Levi asked.

"It's a kind of English coin," Rebecca replied, "like a ten-cent piece, a dime, so Blackstone received about 50 cents in United States money."

Levi asked, "I wish I had 50 cents! But why did he leave Blackstone with less than his sister and brother?"

"We don't know," Rebecca said, "but Grandpa William arranged for Blackstone to have a safe home and a tutor to educate him, so he may have thought that was fair. Caleb was the firstborn and a boy, so he may have been given the land according to English custom.[14] Elizabeth's future husband would expect to receive money to marry her – a dower – from her father, so Grandpa William may have wanted to make sure she had things of value to bring to her husband."

"Did the other Quakers help take care of Blackstone?" Levi asked.

"They would have helped, yes. But they also would have written about any special help they gave or special circumstances, but they didn't write anything down. Still, although the Ingledew children were often sad, they had many friends to help them grow up and be successful in the community," Rebecca replied.

"So, whatever happened to Blackstone?" Levi asked.

Rebecca continued, "Blackstone grew up into a man in County Durham in England. He stayed there until he was almost 30 years old and learned the butcher trade. The Quaker community respected this kind of work. He knew he could find butcher work anywhere. It was during that time when he first married.

"The Stockton Meeting of Quakers approved Blackstone's marriage to Margaret Pattison in 1719,"[15] Rebecca said, "but

---

14   This follows the traditional custom of "primogeniture," where the firstborn child inherits the parent's entire residential estate rather than sharing it among numerous children.

15   Blackstone Ingledew married Margaret Pattison on 14 Apr

she was not 'with child' for five more years, until late 1724. By the time Margaret knew she was going to have a baby, the couple was already planning to go on a big adventure to the New World! They would embark on the long sea voyage thousands of miles across the Atlantic Ocean to a new home in America."

"Why did they want to leave home?" Levi asked.

"Life in England wasn't always easy for Quakers," Rebecca said, "but about 50 years before this time, a Quaker from England named William Penn had gone to America to make a place where Quakers could live in peace. The founder of the Society of Friends, George Fox, had earlier come to Burlington in New Jersey for a visit in 1672. A mass migration promoted by William Penn followed. The king of England owed William Penn's father some money, so the king gave Penn some land in the British colonies in America. Penn came to America and laid out the new City of Philadelphia streets about 100 miles up the Delaware River, where ocean-going ships could dock to bring more Quakers. In 1682, newly arriving Quaker families received free oceanic passage, plus £20 and 500 acres of land. That's where the name for the state of Pennsylvania comes from."

1719. The surname spelled Pattison may be the result of the preference or style of the scribe. It seems more likely that the surname was Patterson.

Rebecca continued the story. "The Quakers organized new Meetings in Philadelphia[16] and the surrounding area. For at least 40 years before Blackstone and Margaret arrived, many Quakers had already made the long and dangerous ocean voyage from England to settle in Philadelphia and the nearby countryside.[17]

"On a brisk day in February 1725," Rebecca said, "Blackstone and Margaret, just three months from having her first baby, walked on wobbly 'sea legs' and stepped onto the pier in the New World!

They'd arrived in Philadelphia after almost two months at sea. Fellow Quakers warmly welcomed them following

---

16   The first Philadelphia Meeting occurred on 9 Jan 1682/83 ("the 9th day of the 11th month … in the year 1682").

17   Ingledue family lore and conventional wisdom are that Blackstone Ingledew was the first Ingledue in North America. However, the First Presbyterian Church in Philadelphia published an index reflecting the marriage of Michael Ingledue and Ruth Drinker on 27 Aug 1702. No other information about either party has been discovered (such as any relationship to Ingledews in England or any of Michael and Ruth's descendants). All other Ingledues found in records in the US from 1725 to 1850 (except one, discussed next) are known to be descendants of Blackstone. The exception is a "Francis Ingledew," with an apparent wife and three children under 16, listed in the 1800 Census in Litchfield, Herkimer County, New York. The 1820 Census finds the couple with no children in Ellisburg, Jefferson County, New York, about 80 miles further northwest of Herkimer County. The 1820 Census also indicates that both of them are still "foreigners, not naturalized," so they would have been relatively recent arrivals because, even after 20 years in the United States, they were still not citizens. Thus, Francis Ingledew could not have been a descendant of Blackstone Ingledew. No other traces of Francis Ingledew or his descendants have been found.

Figure 5: Blackstone and Margaret Ingledew arrive
in Philadelphia in 1725

their introduction in letters sent back to England offering to settle new arrivals."[18]

Rebecca continued, "By 1725, they were not giving Quakers free ocean passage, £20, or 500 acres of land, and Blackstone had spent most of their savings to pay for the ocean passage," Rebecca said. "Still, Blackstone and Margaret were greeted by James and Hannah Parrock, well-known Quakers who had arranged to help the Ingledews settle in Philadelphia. Mr. Parrock was 50 years old and had been born in Philadelphia. Hannah was Mr. Parrock's third wife. His first two wives had died after giving birth to a child, something that still happens sometimes today."

Levi asked, "Do mothers always die after having a baby? Are you going to die?"

Rebecca said, "No, they didn't always die after having a baby, but they sometimes did, and it's still possible sometimes."

"But you won't die, will you, Mama?" Levi asked.

Rebecca answered softly, "God willing, no, Levi," gently pulling him close. "I'll always be with you, but Mamas

18   In a 1997 book, *Hannah: The Story of Hannah Ingledew Janney 1725–1818,* author Polly Grose provides a wonderful dramatization of the story she unearthed after years of research regarding Blackstone's trip to North America, his arrival, and the subsequent life and times of Blackstone's first daughter, Hannah. Ms. Grose's book is now out of print but is available from used book dealers and would be a worthy addition to the library of anyone interested in the early years of the Ingledews in America.

sometimes die, and when they do, they become special angels who watch over their children with love forever and ever."

CHAPTER 3:
GETTING STARTED

"James Parrock was a well-known shipbuilder in Philadelphia who owned a shipyard on the Delaware River at the end of Sassafras Street," Rebecca said. "He built big boats like Grandpa William used to sail. Even though Blackstone didn't follow Grandpa William's career as a mariner, Blackstone grew up in a port city and marveled at those with the skill to build ships. Blackstone and Mr. Parrock quickly became friends, and because of their age difference, Mr. Parrock almost seemed like a father to Blackstone. Mr. Parrock helped Blackstone find a job with Moses Hewes in his grocery store on Chestnut Street.[19]

---

19   See, *Hannah: The Story of Hannah Ingledew Janney 1725–1818*, by Polly Grose.

"One day, Blackstone told Mr. Hewes that he was a butcher, which was a better job than sweeping the floor in the grocery store. Mr. Hewes recommended Blackstone to John Furnis, the son of a barber. John Furnis was a successful butcher whose family had been in Philadelphia for generations. Blackstone began working as a butcher for Mr. Furnis right away.

"When they'd arrived, Blackstone and Margaret moved in with the Parrocks in their residence on Front Street right near the edge of the Delaware River and only about 200 feet from Parrock's shipyard," Rebecca said. "To support his shipbuilding business, Mr. Parrock had purchased a block of lots nearby – houses and shops – mostly on Sassafras Street[20] between Front Street and Second Street. He later sold a house and shop near the corner on Front Street to Blackstone, about 500 feet north of the Friends' old 'Bank Meeting House.'[21] Blackstone seemed to be on the road to business success!"

Rebecca continued, "But family life was more difficult during the first two years in the new world," Rebecca continued. "Soon after Margaret gave birth to Hannah in May 1725, Margaret fell ill and never recovered, leaving

---

20   Sassafras Street is now called Race Street.

21   The Bank Meeting House was built in 1685, but within 15 years (25 years before Blackstone arrived), a new Meeting House was built on the corner of Second and Market Streets about one-third of a mile south from where Blackstone settled soon after arriving.

The 1776 map of Philadelphia (Figure 7 on pages 34-35) depicts the location of three distinct Quaker Meeting Houses (including the Bank Meeting House) plus a Quaker School and the Quaker Alms House, which provided services for the needy.

Figure 6: Bank Meeting House, Front Street, Philadelphia

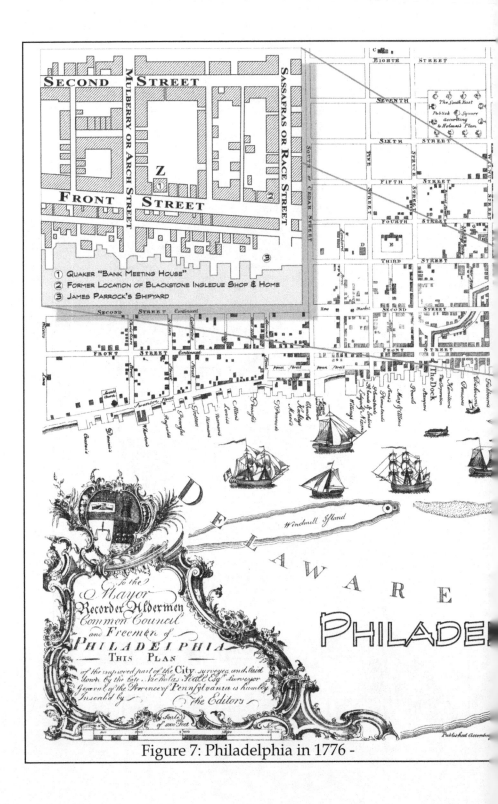

SECOND STREET

MULBERRY OR ARCH STREET

SASSAFRAS OR RACE STREET

Z

FRONT STREET

① QUAKER "BANK MEETING HOUSE"
② FORMER LOCATION OF BLACKSTONE INGLEDUE SHOP & HOME
③ JAMES PARROCK'S SHIPYARD

EIGHTH STREET
SEVENTH
The South East
Publick Square according to Holme's Plan
SIXTH STREET
FIFTH STREET
FOURTH STREET
THIRD STREET
SECOND STREET
FRONT STREET

SECOND STREET Continued
FRONT STREET Continued

The Dock

DELAWARE

Windmill Island

to the
Mayor
Recorder Aldermen
Common Council
and Freemen of
PHILADELPHIA
THIS PLAN
of the improved part of the City surveyed and laid down by the late Nicholas Scull Esqr Surveyor General of the Province of Pennsylvania is humbly Inscrib'd by The Editors

Scale of 2000 Feet

PHILADE

Published According

Figure 7: Philadelphia in 1776 -

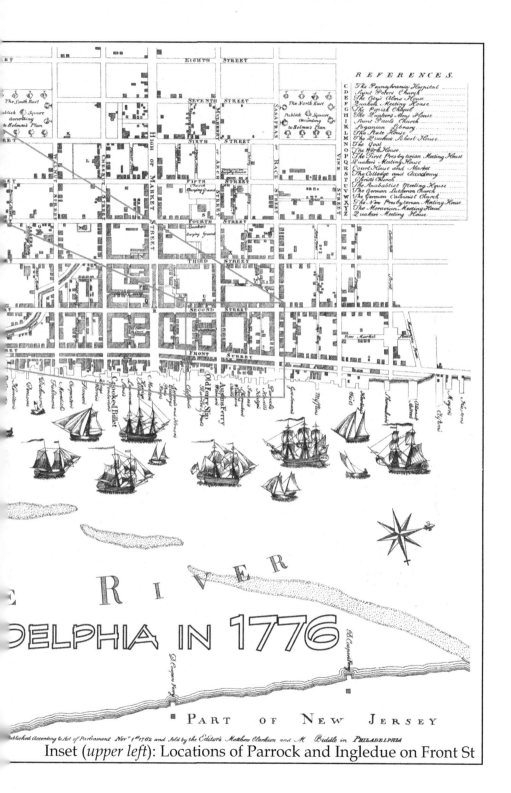

Inset (*upper left*): Locations of Parrock and Ingledue on Front St

Blackstone alone to care for his baby girl, Hannah. By the time Margaret died, Blackstone had become acquainted with Elizabeth Palmer, the daughter of the owner of nearby businesses. Blackstone asked the Philadelphia Meeting of Quakers if he could hire Elizabeth to work in his home to help raise Hannah. The Meeting approved of her employment, and the relationship between Blackstone and Elizabeth soon blossomed into love. The Philadelphia Meeting then approved their marriage."

Rebecca continued, "Blackstone and Elizabeth had their first baby, a son, in 1727. Because he was also named Blackstone, I'll call him Blackstone the Second.[22] He was my grandfather. A daughter, Elizabeth, was born two years later, but she died that same year. They welcomed Margaret and Sarah into the world in 1731 and 1733, so now Blackstone and Elizabeth had a family of three of their own, plus Hannah.[23]

22   Although they did not use conventions such as "Jr," "Sr," or "II," the different Blackstone Ingledues in this book use roman numeral suffixes, e.g., "II" to identify the son of Blackstone, III for the grandson of Blackstone, etc. The timeline below should help clarify who the different Blackstones were and when they lived.

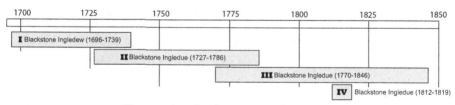

Figure 8: Blackstone Life Spans

23   The children of Blackstone Ingledew identified here are those known to exist by independent records. Volume II of *Hinshaw's Encyclopedia of American Quaker Genealogy* contains a reference on page 380 to a "William Ingledue, son of Blackstone, buried in Philadelphia 1-14-1731." Still, this William's birth is not recorded, so he was apparently an infant who died soon after being born. Additionally,

"But it almost seemed like Blackstone was cursed because Elizabeth died when Sarah was only two years old in October 1735," Rebecca explained. "Blackstone remarried a year later to Mary Wright in New Jersey. Mary wasn't a Quaker, and we only know they had no children.

"Hannah was only ten years old when her stepmother, Elizabeth, died, just a little older than you are today," Rebecca said, "so she was forced to grow up quickly, helping her father care for her three sisters and her brother, Blackstone the Second. Blackstone (the First)'s heart broke when Elizabeth died. He became sick more often. On September 19, 1739, four years after his wife Elizabeth died, Blackstone also passed away aged 43. Hannah was only 14 years old but would soon be old enough to marry.

"To make matters worse," Rebecca added, "Blackstone's businesses didn't thrive. So Blackstone didn't have any money to leave in a will to provide for his children the way Grandpa William had done for his children. Blackstone died poor with four under-aged children, owing other people more than his property was worth. Within a year, the court ordered his properties sold to pay the money he owed others.[24] When it was all over, the children had no money left. A judge decided the fate of Blackstone's four children in 'Orphans Court.'

---

some family trees show an Alice Ingledue born about 1730, but there does not appear to be any reliable birth or death record for Alice.

24   Blackstone died intestate (without a will) in substantial debt to James Parrock, William Tidmarsh, and others.

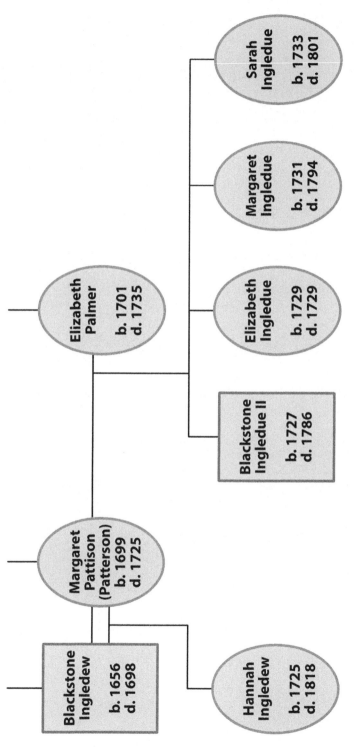

Figure 9: Early 18th Century Blackstone Ingledew, wives, and children

"We don't know all the details of what happened in Orphans Court in 1740, but Elizabeth Palmer's family, also Quakers, had roots in Bucks County, just north of Philadelphia," Rebecca said. "We believe all four children – Hannah, Blackstone the Second, Margaret, and Sarah – went to Bucks County to live with Elizabeth's relatives, Jonathan and David Palmer.

"On March 20, 1742, two months before her 17th birthday, Hannah received permission to marry from the Fallsington Meeting of Quakers in Bucks County," Rebecca said. "Hannah married Jacob Janney, a member of a well-known Quaker family who arrived in Philadelphia with many other Quakers aboard a ship called *Endeavor* on September 29, 1683, and quickly settled on a 300-acre farm in Makefield Township in Bucks County, Pennsylvania. Jacob's grandfather Thomas Janney was a Quaker minister who brought his whole family from Cheshire, England, to America as part of a large Quaker migration that began arriving in 1682 on a fleet of ships paid for by William Penn."

Rebecca continued, "Jacob was 14 years older than Hannah. But it was the first marriage for both of them. Within months of their marriage, Jacob and Hannah moved 250 miles south to live near other members of Jacob's family who had bought land in Loudoun County, Virginia. Before the end of that year, Hannah had given birth to the first of her 12 children."

"Why did Hannah move so far away from Blackstone and her sisters?" Levi asked.

"Besides being good Quakers, the Janney family were industrious farmers," said Rebecca. "They'd heard of better farming land in the south. The governor of Virginia had approved a new settlement in Virginia that had been requested by about 70 Quaker families, including Jacob's. The Goose Creek Meeting of Quakers in Loudoun County was formally established soon after Jacob and Hannah Janney arrived."[25]

"Whatever happened to Hannah?" Levi asked.

"She lived the life of a perfect Quaker and was able to teach many others in the ways of the Society of Friends," Rebecca said. "She died 31 years ago in 1818 at the advanced age of 92 years. She was such a respected and well-known Quaker that the Goose Creek Meeting included a long memorial about her in their minutes."[26]

"Did Blackstone, Margaret, and Sarah stay behind with the Palmers after Jacob and Hannah went to Goose Creek?" asked Levi.

---

25   A *different* Goose Creek Meeting in Virginia was established years later, in 1794, further south in Bedford County. There are indications of a small presence of Ingledues in the Goose Creek Meeting, Bedford County.

26   After Hannah died on 23 Feb 1818, the Goose Creek Meeting appointed a committee to prepare a testimonial remembering Hannah. This testimonial was some five pages long and was included in the record of the Annual Baltimore Meeting.

"Yes, they were too young to go on their own," Rebecca said, "so they stayed in Bucks County with the Palmers. But then – finally – something wonderful happened to this family! In 1746, the Palmers received word that their aunt Elizabeth, their father Blackstone's sister back in England, had died and left a great deal of money to young Blackstone the Second and his sisters Margaret and Sarah. The Palmers received permission from Orphans Court to accept the inheritance and use it for the children's benefit. Their lives and outlook improved, and they grew up as Quakers in Bucks County with the Palmers."

CHAPTER 4:
MORE
INGLEDUE MIGRATION

"One by one, over the next 15 years, each of the three children of Blackstone Ingledue and Elizabeth Palmer followed their sister Hannah south to Goose Creek," Rebecca said.

"Since Blackstone the Second was the last to travel south, but also because he's your direct ancestor, I'll tell you about his path to Goose Creek after I tell you about Margaret and Sarah," Rebecca continued.

"About two years after the inheritance from Aunt Elizabeth arrived from England, Margaret was 17 years old. In several letters sent back home to Bucks County, Hannah pleaded with

Margaret to visit her in Loudoun County.[27] Margaret finally came in 1749. Soon after Margaret arrived at Hannah's, a Quaker man bothered her. The Quaker Meeting punished him[28] and Margaret never married. She lived as a good Quaker in Goose Creek until she died aged 63.[29]

"Sarah followed her sister to Loudoun County eight years after Margaret, when she was 24. The Middletown Meeting in Bucks County granted her a certificate to help her acceptance as a member of the Goose Creek Meeting in Loudoun County.[30] Six months later, the Goose Creek Meeting gave final approval for Sarah to marry[31] John Hatcher,[32] a local landowner. Mr. Hatcher had a brother, William, who became an important part of our story. Sarah had five babies

---

27   It is only speculation that Hannah wrote several letters pleading with her sister Margaret to visit her in Loudoun County. Still, the record is clear that Margaret eventually moved close to Hannah in Loudoun County. It seems unlikely that was a coincidental choice.

28   On 29 Jul 1749, the Fairfax Monthly Meeting (near Goose Creek) investigated Margaret's complaint that Joseph Harris had attempted to violate her chastity. After an investigation by the Monoquesey Meeting, the Meeting disowned Harris but said they were "hoping he may return to us for his soul's sake."

29   Margaret died on 5 Mar 1794, and is buried at the Friends Burying Ground at Goose Creek, in Lincoln, in Loudoun County, Virginia. The Friends Ground is on land donated to the Meeting by John Hatcher, the husband of Margaret's sister, Sarah.

30   The Middletown Meeting granted Sarah's certificate on 4 Nov 1756.

31   The Goose Creek Meeting approved Sarah's marriage on 30 Apr 1757.

32   William Hatcher was born in 1746 in Bucks County, Pennsylvania, and died in Goose Creek, Loudoun County, Virginia, in December 1816.

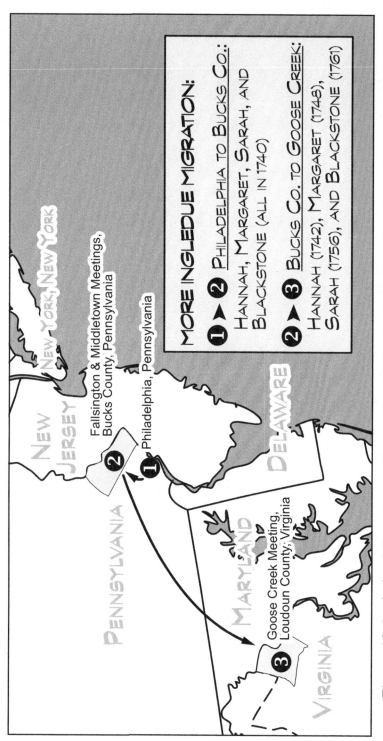

Figure 10: Ingledue Migration to Goose Creek Monthly Meeting, Loudoun County, Virginia

with Mr. Hatcher. She stayed in Loudoun County with Mr. Hatcher until she died almost 50 years ago, in 1801.

"Blackstone the Second, remained in Bucks County five years longer than Sarah, until 1761," Rebecca continued. "Blackstone was in Pennsylvania during a time of military conflict, but it was well before the Revolutionary War.[33] We don't know what prompted him to do so, but at some time before May 1759, Blackstone enlisted in the military and went off to war, probably in western Pennsylvania where the French were trying to take land that is now Ohio. When he returned, however, the Falls Meeting of Quakers found out Blackstone had enlisted as a soldier. They pleaded with him and gave him time to correct himself, but he wouldn't. They

---

33   The government in Pennsylvania had a difficult time organizing a militia because Quakers made up a majority of the Assembly and were pacifists. Benjamin Franklin had become increasingly concerned about the ability of the colony to defend itself against attacks from the French, so he created a militia bill that the Assembly passed in November 1755. The bill passed by the Assembly sanctioned a series of local militias organized by county whereby each militia "associated" with the other. The men in these militias were all volunteers called "Associators," but they had to bring their own firearms and ammunition. It was also established that they would never be away from their homes for more than three days. But Quakers were not allowed to take the new oaths of office being required for elected officials by the militia act or required of those who served in the association, even voluntarily. In 1756, word reached the colony that the king of England had vetoed the Associator system because its all-volunteer nature allowed men to shirk what he deemed to be their responsibility.

By March 1759, a series of battles in western Pennsylvania during what is now called the French and Indian War – combined with the loss of the Quaker majority in the Assembly – proved sufficient motivation for the Assembly to establish a provincial militia that could be dispatched for conflict anywhere in Pennsylvania.

disowned him from the Society of Friends a few months later, so he was no longer a Quaker.[34]

"Soon afterwards, Blackstone the Second moved to Virginia. There he met a pretty girl who was 20 years old, Ann Rue. Ann wasn't a Quaker. Her family belonged to the Dutch Reformed Church, and she and her family didn't care that the Quakers had disowned Blackstone for enlisting in a militia. After courting her for over a year, Blackstone married Ann in her family's church."[35]

---

34   On 2 May 1759, the Falls Monthly Meeting investigated Blackstone II: *"Blackstone Ingledue who was born of parents professing with Friends, some time since enlisted himself a soldier in the forces raised in this province, and continued so during the [campaign], and since his return has been treated with by the overseers but does not seem properly disposed to make any acknowledgment."* Over the summer, the Meeting investigated this report and attempted to get Blackstone II to repent, but he did not cooperate. He was disowned for "disunity" on 4 Sep 1759. These events, supported by multiple Quaker records, appear to be the only documents reflecting a circumstance where any Blackstone Ingledue was ever disowned by the Quakers for any kind of military activity. This is a relevant fact because modern Ingledue family lore embraces a story that a Blackstone Ingledue was "running guns" on ships he owned or operated during the Revolutionary War. Apart from the lack of any documentary record supporting this family lore, the story does not add up because:

- Blackstone II was already disowned in 1759, well before the Revolutionary War.

- Blackstone II was 50 years old when the Revolutionary War began and died in 1786, so he was unlikely to be involved in any "warmongering" during the Revolutionary War.

- Blackstone II was not wealthy and owned no ships to run guns with, even if he wanted to.

- Blackstone III was born about 1770, six years before the Revolution and was not a Quaker.

35   Blackstone married Ann Rue on 20 May 1761.

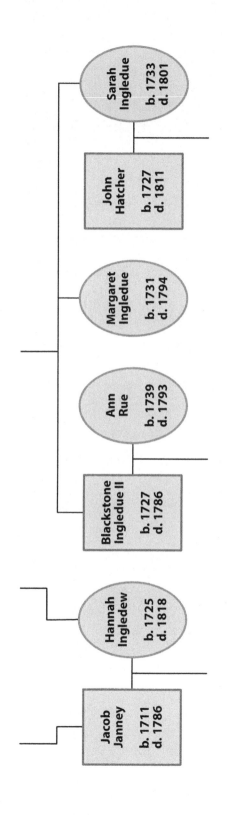

Figure 11: Children of Blackstone Ingledue and their spouses

Rebecca continued, "By 1770, Blackstone had been married to Ann Rue for nine years and had joined all his sisters in Loudoun County," Rebecca continued. "We don't know why, but Blackstone and Ann didn't begin their family until that time when Ann was 31 years old. Hannah, Margaret, and Sarah remained in Loudoun County for their lifetimes. But Blackstone and Ann would migrate west in the years to come."

CHAPTER 5:
THE NEXT GENERATION

Rebecca explained that although Blackstone and Ann lived in the vicinity of Quakers during their married life, "They were not Quakers, nor were their children. But they were not 'shunned' by Quakers either. They lived near and around Quakers like the Janneys and the Hatchers."[36]

---

36   The available record reflects close relationships between the Ingledues and the Quakers in the communities surrounding them. For example, several documents show Janneys and Hatchers "near" those for Blackstone Ingledue II in the Loudoun County Tithe (tax) list from 1770 to 1784. Although the Loudoun County Tithable Lists were not organized entirely by geography, the payment of taxes was an in-person event recorded by a local official who recorded the taxes paid in the order that citizens presented themselves. In this case, there are numerous instances over a 14-year period where Blackstone's name appears in the Shelbourne Parish lists with Hatchers and Janneys (both Quaker families) immediately preceding or following Blackstone on the list, suggesting they traveled together in a small group to the place they were called to pay their taxes.

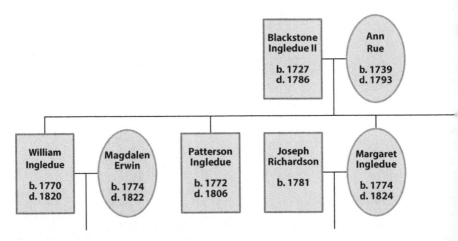

Figure 12: Children of Blackstone Ingledue II and ...

She continued. "While living amongst Quakers in Loudoun County, Blackstone and Ann had six children from 1770 to 1780, during the same time the United States declared independence from England! The names of the six children," Rebecca explained, "in the order they were born, were William, Patterson, Margaret, Blackstone the Third, Ebener, and Ann."

Rebecca continued, "Blackstone the Second died in Loudoun County in 1786, leaving all six under-age children in the care of his wife, Ann, who didn't have enough money to care for them all," Rebecca explained. "William was 17 years old the next year, 1787, when he agreed to help by being 'bound out' by the Overseers of the Poor to Stacey Taylor as a servant to learn how to be a carpenter. William's little brother, Ebener, was only ten years old in 1787 when the Overseers of the Poor also bound him to be a servant in the home of Richard Brown.

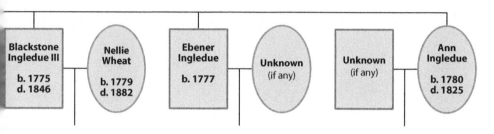

... Ann Rue and their spouses

"Ann still had four young mouths to feed, but she did her best." Rebecca continued, "In 1792, six years after her husband, Blackstone, died, she asked the Overseers of the Poor to place her youngest child, Ann Ingledue, then 12 years old, as a servant in the home of Blackstone's brother-in-law, William Hatcher, and his wife, Mary. Ann may have already been living with the Hatcher family when, in 1793, the Overseers of the Poor approved her mother's request. Sadly, her mother died later that same year, just after her daughter Ann had officially begun living with the Hatchers.

"By the time his mother, Ann, died in 1793," Rebecca said, "Patterson was 21 years old and able to support himself. Margaret was 19 years old, and Joseph Richardson was courting her. Blackstone the Third was 17 years old and had to use his wits and strong work ethic to make his way into the world, but it appears he migrated with his brother William to Bedford County, Virginia, and beyond."

Rebecca explained that "Each of Blackstone the Second's children grew up, but not all of them married. Patterson Ingledue was born in 1772, but we don't think he ever married or had children. Ebener may have married, but we lost track of him after he was bound out to Mr. Brown in 1787."

Levi asked, "Where did they all go after their mother died?"

Rebecca gave Levi a summary followed by some detail on each child.

"After completing his term of service as a carpenter with Stacey Taylor, William traveled south to a Quaker Meeting that was growing in Bedford County, Virginia, called the South River Meeting. It can be confusing, but the South River Meeting was later called the Goose Creek Monthly Meeting."

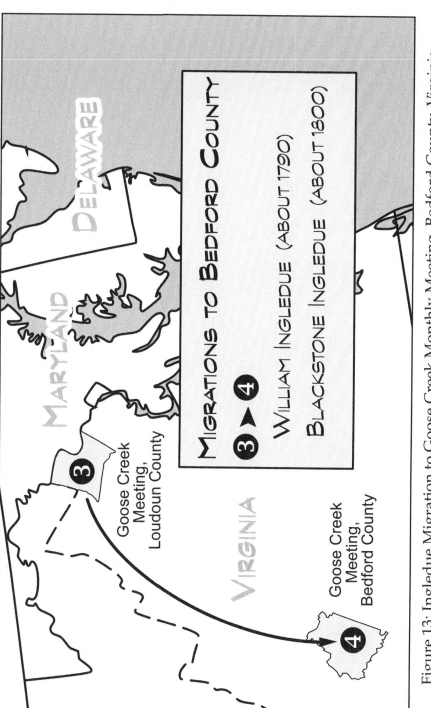

Figure 13: Ingledue Migration to Goose Creek Monthly Meeting, Bedford County, Virginia

Rebecca continued, "We don't know much about Margaret Ingledue except that she married Joseph Richardson, who came from Bucks County in Pennsylvania. She and Mr. Richardson had at least two sons, Rue Richardson and Harvey Richardson. In 1823, her sister, Ann, identified Margaret in her will to receive money with payments scheduled through 1830. We think Margaret died around 1830, but we don't know where she rests.

"As I said, we don't know what became of Ebener after he was bound out to Mr. Brown," she said. "That leaves us with Blackstone the Third and Ann Ingledue.

"Before I tell you about Blackstone and his sister, Ann," Rebecca said, "I need to tell you a little more about William Ingledue because he and his wife had many children. I used to live with some of them. Some of them even live around here!"

"Who lives around here?" Levi asked with excitement.

"Well," Rebecca said, "I'll tell you, but it'll help to know how they got here and how they are related to you, so I'll tell you more about William now.

"William had traveled to Bedford County after working for Mr. Taylor. It was there he met his bride, Magdalen Erwin. Magdalen was 20 years old and was a Quaker, but William wasn't. Magdalen was a member of the South River Monthly Meeting of the Quakers. They were married in

1794[37] by a Justice of the Peace but didn't have approval from the Meeting. When the Elders at the South River Meeting found out that Magdalen had married William, they ruled that Magdalen Erwin could no longer be a Quaker because she married 'contrary to discipline,' and they disowned her.[38]

"Magdalen had been a good Quaker and was very sad to lose her standing in the Society of Friends, but she loved William and knew beforehand what might happen if she married William. She still hoped to be someday restored as a Quaker, so she continued living in the Quaker community according to their morals. About 15 years after she married William, she began seeking reinstatement as a Quaker at the Middleton Monthly Meeting in Columbiana County, Ohio. But the Middleton Monthly Meeting had heard about her being disowned for her 'contrary to discipline' in Virginia. They made her wait two more years before they finally readmitted her."[39]

---

37   William Ingledue married Magdalen Erwin on 21 Jul 1794.

38   Magdalen was disowned on 20 Sep 1794.

39   On 5 Jul 1810, the leaders of the Goose Creek Meeting in Bedford County, Virginia, handled a request for information from the Middleton Monthly Meeting in Columbiana County regarding Magdalen's request for reinstatement as a Quaker in Ohio. The Goose Creek Meeting reported to the Middleton Monthly Meeting that the nearby South River Meeting had disowned Magdalen for marrying William Ingledue contrary to discipline.

On 9 Nov 1811, the South River Meeting back in Bedford County, Virginia, considered Magdalene's renewed request for reinstatement at the Middleton Monthly Meeting.

On 11 Jun 1812, the Middleton Monthly Meeting finally received Magdalen Ingledue back into the Society of Friends.

Rebecca continued, "Blackstone the Third, also traveled south from Loudoun to Bedford County. In 1803, in Bedford County, Blackstone the Third married Nellie Wheat,[40] who had come to Bedford County from Maryland with her parents. Neither were Quakers, and they were married by a Baptist minister, Jeremiah Hatcher. Blackstone and Nellie had several children, including Blackstone Ingledue, the Fourth, but he died when he was seven years old.[41]

"Ann lived in Loudon County for the rest of her life, just like her sister Sarah. Ann continued to work in William Hatcher's home until Mr. Hatcher died in 1816. I was only eight years old when he died, the same age you are today. In his will, Mr. Hatcher left Ann Ingledue, then 36 years old,

---

40   Blackstone III was married to Nellie Wheat on 28 Sep 1803, by Reverend Jeremiah Hatcher who, in 1803, had been in Bedford County for over 20 years. It is unknown what relationship Jeremiah Hatcher had with John Hatcher, Sarah Ingledue's husband.

41   Although it cannot be discounted, one theory might be that Rebecca Ingledue was an undocumented daughter of Blackstone III and Nellie Wheat. According to Rebecca's age at death (41 yrs) on her gravestone, she was born between 20 Jul 1807 and 19 Jul 1808. If she had been conceived nine months before the later date, that conception would have been 19 Nov 1807. The problem with that fact is it all but rules out Nellie as Rebecca's mother because Nellie gave birth to Eber Rue Ingledue less than three weeks prior on 31 Oct 1807. Additionally, there is ample documentation of the existence and lives of Blackstone III's other children, so the theory that Rebecca was born without any record and then disconnected from the family is a theory that strains credulity.

$100 because he said she'd been a good girl to him.[42] Ann died seven years later, about 30 years ago."

Seeing a change in his mother's face, Levi asked, "Mama, why are you sad?"

Rebecca, whose eyes were becoming filled with tears, quietly said, "Because Ann was my Mama, and I miss her." She paused and looked at Levi. He looked back at her with all the compassion and love his young heart could release. She felt that love, so she continued. "My Mama wasn't married when she had me in 1808. I never knew who my father was."

"Just like me," said Levi quickly.

Rebecca smiled again, reflecting on her perceptive young son, and continued, "Yes, Levi, in many ways, that's true." She smiled again. "Mr. Hatcher had been a nice man to my Mama and allowed her to keep me with her while she lived with the Hatchers and took care of his house. Mr. Hatcher's wife, Mary, had died in 1801, so Mama had plenty of work. But when Mr. Hatcher died, and I was still only eight years old, Mama didn't have a proper place to live. Mama wasn't sure if she could provide a good home for me, so she sent me to live with family in Columbiana County.

---

42   In his last will and testament, executed on 14 Nov 1816, William Hatcher Jr. first bequeathed his married sister $50. But then he deeded, "to my present housekeeper Anne Ingledue who has been a good girl to me, the sum of one hundred dollars" while his remaining assets were to be liquidated and given to the children of his other sisters and brothers. William Hatcher Jr's only son, born on 27 May 1765, was apparently alive in 1816 but was not mentioned in his father's will.

"It was a very tearful goodbye. I never saw my Mama again, but I always remember her. After many years, I came to believe what she told me – again and again – before I went away: 'It's for the best. It's for the best.' My Mama stayed in Loudoun County and sent money when she could to the family in Columbiana County. After Mama died, my aunt, Margaret, began sending money when she could to help William and Magdalen take care of me."[43]

---

43   This story, that Rebecca's mother was an unmarried Ann Ingledue, is the best possible theory. No facts have been discovered to contradict it, but this conclusion may not yet meet all the proof standards for professional genealogical research. While the author has uncovered numerous facts and DNA evidence leaving no reasonable doubt that Rebecca was Levi's mother, the same cannot conclusively be said as to Ann Ingledue being Rebecca's mother. The conclusion that Rebecca was Ann's daughter relies upon careful examination of all existing Ingledues and associated family units, diligent analysis of every other potential parent of Rebecca Ingledue, and exclusion of all other possibilities (e.g. impossible due to existing families, pregnancies, children, etc.).

Also, although William Hatcher's wife Mary died in 1801, there is no support for a theory that William was Rebecca's father. There are no documents or DNA matches supporting a theory that William Hatcher could have been Rebecca's father in 1808. Still, the reflection of William in his will is curious, where he wrote that Ann had been a "good girl to him." However, there is no group of DNA matches of Levi's descendants that match with known descendants of William Hatcher or his close relations. Additionally, Ann Ingledue died with an estate of about $600 ($500 more than William had bequeathed to her). In her will, Ann gave about 75% of that $600 to her sister Margaret. Margaret was married and probably did not need the money, certainly not in an amount disproportionate to that Ann bequeathed to her brother Blackstone. Rebecca may never have been told who her father was, leaving her with a sad emptiness in her own story. These circumstances may explain why Rebecca understood, deep down, that it would be important – at some point – for her own child to know who his father was.

CHAPTER 6:
WEST TO OHIO

Levi asked his mother to tell him why the family had moved to Columbiana County and from where, so Rebecca continued.

"My Mama's sister Margaret stayed in Loudoun County, but remember that her brother, my uncle William, moved southwest into Bedford County in Virginia. It was a sad time for William and Magdalen after the Quakers disowned Magdalen. However, even Magdalen's family (who were still Quakers) could see William and Magdalen loved each other. William and Magdalen had heard about new land in northeastern Ohio. William and Magdalen decided to move there to start a new life in 1803, when they'd been married only nine years. It was a difficult decision, but they moved."

"How far was it from Bedford County to Columbiana?" Levi asked.

"It's about 400 miles, and it took them a month to get there by horse and wagon over the Appalachian Mountains. Because it was such a long journey, and for safety on the trail, they traveled in a large group of families making the same move. They traveled a well-worn path, staying with friends and relatives along the way, people who had previously settled in the countryside they passed through on their way west."

"What did they do when they arrived in Columbiana?" Levi asked.

"They were welcomed by friends who had arrived before them who helped them find land they could buy and develop into farms. William, Magdalen, and her brother, Samuel Erwin, all settled in the east part of Columbiana County in Fairfield Township."

Rebecca continued, "In 1805, a couple of years after William and Magdalen moved to Columbiana County, William's brother, Patterson Ingledue, migrated west from Goose Creek and settled in Ohio County, near Wheeling along the Ohio River, in what is now West Virginia. He died there after a tragic accident in 1806."[44]

44   Patterson died in a tragic accident at 33 years of age near Wheeling, on the Ohio river, the border between Ohio and West Virginia. In November 1805, Patterson signed a 7-month contract to operate a grist mill and farm for Archibald Woods, a local landowner. However, Patterson was killed two months later when a tree fell on him. Two relatives attended to his estate: Patterson's brother William

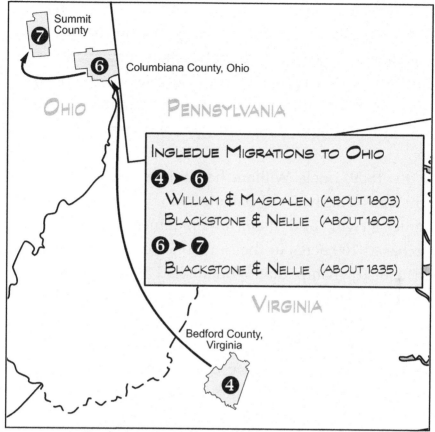

Figure 14: Ingledue Migrations to Ohio

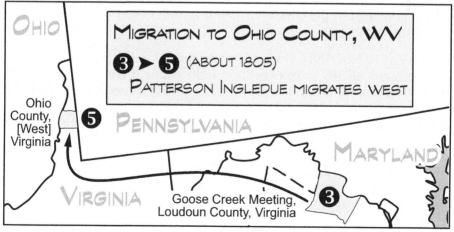

Figure 15: Patterson Ingledue Migration to Ohio County, West Virginia

"Around that same time," Rebecca said, "my uncle Blackstone the Third, and his family followed William and Magdalen to Columbiana County, where they lived for many years before buying land about 50 miles west in Summit County. So, by 1815, several Ingledue families and their relatives had migrated from Virginia and were living in Ohio.

"By 1809, uncle William had purchased 60 acres about eight miles southeast of Salem, Ohio.[45] Magdalen's brother, Samuel Erwin, and their father, James Erwin, had each purchased 160 acres in the same one-square-mile section of Fairfield Township that William had bought. Around the same time, another large family, the Cooks, migrated from Pennsylvania and settled about ten miles northwest of uncle William in Green Township, about five miles northeast of Salem. The Cooks were a prosperous family who laid out and sold plots in a new community called Green Village."[46]

– who was living 75 miles north in Fairfield Township, Columbiana County, Ohio – and Patterson's cousin, Joshua Hatcher (son of John Hatcher and Sarah Ingledue), who had five years earlier purchased a land patent from the US Government 20 miles west in Belmont County, Ohio.

45   On 10 Nov 1807, Daniel Stratton purchased, from the US Government, all 360 acres of Section 12 in Fairfield Township in Columbiana County, Ohio, pursuant to a patent issued by President Thomas Jefferson. Daniel Stratton began selling subdivided parcels to others. On 28 Mar 1809, William Ingledue paid $180 for one such parcel, 60 acres of on the northeast corner of Section 12. On the same day, William's brother-in-law, Samuel Erwin, purchased the 160 acres making up the northwest quarter of Section 12, and his father-in-law, James Erwin, purchased the 160 acres making up the southwest quarter of Section 12.

46   This community became known as Greenford around 1875, named after a railroad station on the main east-west road.

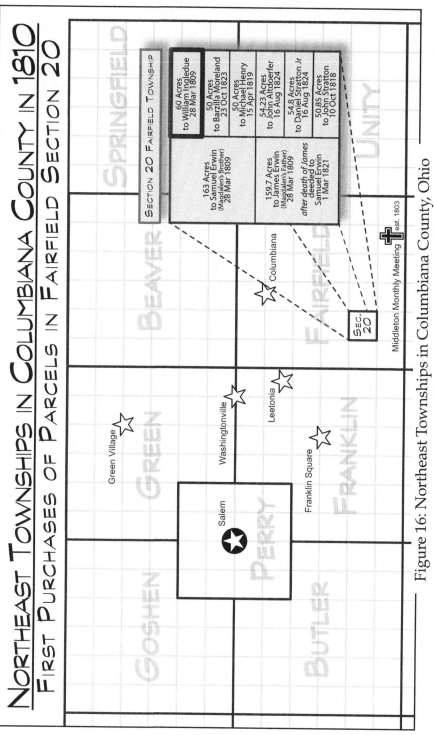

Figure 16: Northeast Townships in Columbiana County, Ohio

"Why did you mention the Cooks? Are they important to this story?" Levi asked.

"Yes, dear, they are important, but I need to finish this part first," Rebecca answered. "My uncle William was a good man. He and Magdalen lived within the Quaker community in Fairfield Township. Still, Magdalen hadn't yet been accepted into the Middleton Monthly Meeting, whose Meeting House was only four miles east of their home. Finally, in 1812, the Middleton Monthly Meeting restored Magdalen as a member of the Society."

"Besides William being your uncle, what does all this mean?" Levi asked.

Rebecca answered, "When my Mama needed to send me away after Mr. Hatcher died, uncle William and Magdalen agreed to give me a home in Ohio.[47] Magdalen had been accepted into the Society of Friends four years earlier, so she was honored to help my mother and me as well as raise her own children as Quakers. When I arrived, I was about your

---

47   It is only a theory that Rebecca's first home in Ohio was with William and Magdalen Ingledue in Columbiana County. The US Census did not attempt to individually enumerate residents until 1850. Prior to that, the Census reflected the name of the head of household, usually a man, and then a count of people in pre-set age ranges. Even with families with children of known ages, such Census sheets are not reliable. In other words, there is no 1830 Census reflecting someone Rebecca's age added to the existing home of William and Magdalen Ingledue. In any case, it seems unlikely that Rebecca would have independently found her way west from Virginia all the way to Allen County, Ohio, if she was not already accepted as a member of William Ingledue's family, where their daughter, Elizabeth Ingledue (just a few years older than Rebecca), married Jacob Cook and others migrated from Columbiana County through Allen County as far west as Iowa.

age, just eight years old. They already had seven children, all my cousins, including their youngest, also named William, who was my age. As I got older, I began helping more and more around the house."

Rebecca continued, "Even though I missed my Mama, it became a happy time. I became very close to all my cousins, including Lewis and Elizabeth, who were four or five years older than me and helped me learn the ways of the farm. My cousins and I helped with chores like milking the cows, cleaning the stalls, and collecting eggs, but a farmer always needs help from the men in the community for the big things like clearing land, raising barns, and harvesting crops. So we got to visit with many people in the area as our family helped them, and they helped us."

"Why did it take so many people?" Levi asked.

"Most of that land, and even this land around us," Rebecca explained, while extending her arm to point out to the surrounding fields, "was a forest when they arrived. They had to cut down trees, use oxen to pull stumps, and cut and mill the trees into lumber to build houses and barns, all before they could ever plant crops. Some men ran lumber mills, some were builders, some were farmers, but they all worked together to build a thriving community, just like they still do here in Allen County."

Levi asked for confirmation, "They still do that around here?"

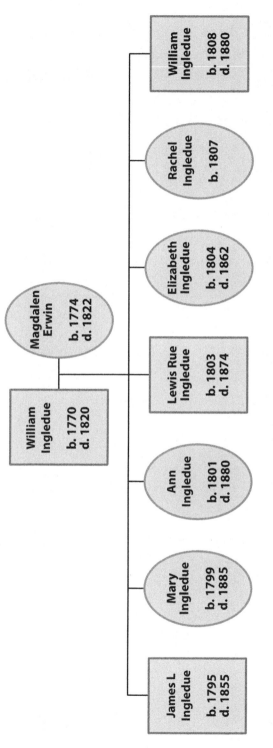

Figure 17: William Ingledue & Magdalen Erwin and children

"Yes, Levi," she said, "Papa Dawson and his family got much of his land from the government and then cleared and developed it. Back then, the government issued what they called patents to people who wanted to settle on what was then the western frontier. The people had to pay the government for the land, but it wasn't as expensive as buying a farm that someone had already developed."

Levi said, "So all this land around here came from people buying government patents?"

DUCHOUQUET, UNION, AND WAYNE
KEY PATENT PURCHASES

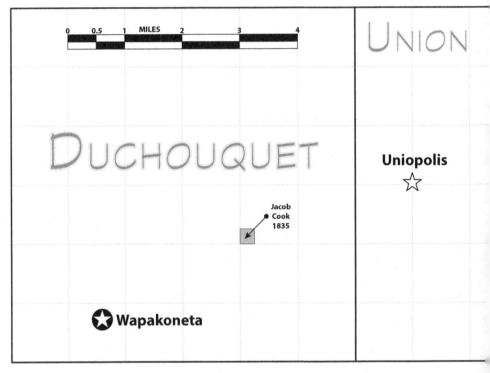

Figure 18: Duchouquet, ...   Union, and ...

Rebecca answered, "Yes. Papa Dawson and his family bought some early patents. Still, in 1835, Jacob Cook, one of the Cooks from Columbiana County, also purchased a patent for 40 acres near Wapakoneta, about 12 miles west of where we're sitting right now. He and his wife moved there and built their homestead."

Levi asked, "You mentioned the Cooks again. Can you tell me why?"

TOWNSHIPS IN ALLEN/AUGLAIZE COUNTIES AND CEMETERY LOCATIONS

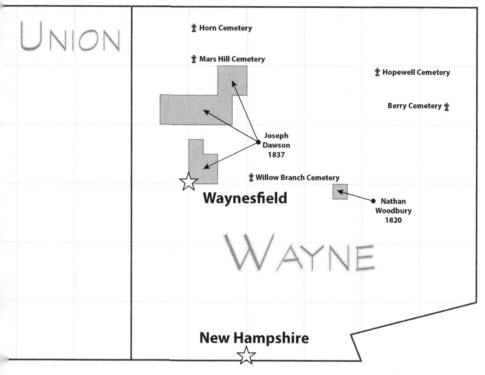

... Wayne Townships in Allen/Auglaize Counties, Ohio

Rebecca lowered her voice and said, "Yes. But, before talking about the Cooks, I wanted to make sure you understood the other families and where they came from. I will tell you about the Cooks now."

CHAPTER 7:
JACOB COOK AND ELIZABETH INGLEDUE

"My cousin, Elizabeth Ingledue, was 12 years old when I came to live with her and her family in Columbiana County," Rebecca said. "Her mother was trying to raise her as a Quaker, but Elizabeth hadn't requested admission into the Meeting like her sisters. Still, she was older than me and could help cook and serve food and refreshments to the men who gathered for construction or farm work."

Levi asked, "How many men were around to help?"

"It depended on what they were doing," Rebecca said, "but it wasn't unusual to have 20 men to complete the work much faster. All that hard work made for hungry men. It was at one of these gatherings that Elizabeth first met Jacob Cook.

He was only two years older than Elizabeth. Jacob's family had come to Ohio with money from back East.

"In 1823, when she wasn't quite 20 years old, my cousin Elizabeth married Jacob Cook in a civil ceremony. Five years before Jacob and Elizabeth married, her sisters Ann, Mary, and even her 11-year-old sister, Rachel, were already members of the Middleton Monthly Meeting. Jacob Cook wasn't a Quaker, and Elizabeth hadn't asked to be received by the Middleton Monthly Meeting like her sisters, so Jacob and Elizabeth were free to be married by a Justice of the Peace."

Rebecca continued, "In 1819, four years before Jacob and Elizabeth married, and when Jacob was only 17 years old, Jacob had paid $700 to buy 160 acres of land about five miles northeast of Salem, Ohio. Just a couple years after marrying Elizabeth, Jacob and two other men bought some additional land nearby and laid out a new town they called Green Village.[48] They began selling small lots in the center of this new village.

"Six years into their marriage, in 1829, Jacob and Elizabeth had sold the first of many lots in Green Village (see Figure 16 on page 71), while Jacob looked west for new opportunities. They continued to sell lots in Green Village for almost 20 years, but about 15 years ago, Jacob and Elizabeth headed west to settle in Duchouquet Township in what is now Auglaize County, Ohio. In October 1835, Jacob and Elizabeth bought a patent for a 40-acre parcel about three miles northeast of

---

48   This community became known as Greenford around 1875.

Wapakoneta, just ten miles west of where we sit today.

"When the Cooks began moving west in 1834, my cousin Elizabeth was still having babies and knew that they would need help resettling 200 miles to the west, so she asked me if I'd come along to help," Rebecca explained. "I went with them to help them settle in Allen County. I helped take care of their growing family and settle into the home they built see a way out, but I knew I had to try at least to go my own there.[49] They sold the last of their Green Village lots in 1839, two years before you were born.

"By then, I was 31 years old, what many called an 'old maid' because I'd never married. Like my mother, it seems that I'd been very busy taking care of other people and their children instead of seeking a life of my own. It was hard to way. That year, some men in Union Township in what was then Allen County laid out a new town they called Uniopolis and began selling lots the same way I'd seen Jacob Cook do to create Green Village back in Columbiana County. Uniopolis was about three miles east of Jacob and Elizabeth Cook's

49   The story that Rebecca lived with the Cooks for any period is speculation based upon: (1) in 1839, Rebecca purchased a lot in Uniopolis, a new town laid out about three miles east of the Cook homestead and about six miles west of Waynesfield, home to many Dawsons, (2) Ann Ingledue had been a caretaker in another man's home while Rebecca was present to see that type of work in practice, and (3) DNA evidence demonstrates that Jacob Cook was Levi Ingledue's biological father. The last fact puts Jacob Cook and Rebecca Ingledue in personal contact in mid-January 1841, two weeks before Jacob's wife Elizabeth gave birth to Malissa Cook on 28 Jan 1841. Additionally, Elizabeth subsequently became pregnant with Thomas J. Cook just three months after Malissa was born (Thomas J. Cook was born on 26 Jan 1842).

homestead. Waynesfield was six miles further east from Uniopolis. I bought one of the lots in Uniopolis and dreamed of building a cottage of my own there. To help save money for my own house, I took a job in Waynesfield working for Papa Dawson, who said he would pay me to help with his children after his wife had died."

"Is that when you came to Papa Dawson? Before you married him?" Levi asked.

"Yes, Levi," Rebecca said, "Papa Dawson could see I was a good person who knew how to keep house but could also see I wanted to become independent from the Cooks. I began working for Papa Dawson in 1839 after the Cooks established their new homestead. But I continued to travel back and forth to visit and help my cousin Elizabeth."

"How did you get there? Wasn't that very far away?" Levi asked.

"If I couldn't find a neighbor taking their horse and buggy to Wapakoneta, I'd start walking," Rebecca said, "but it was a busy road, and people always stopped to offer me a ride. It would usually take me about two hours each way."

"How long did you continue to travel between the Cooks and the Dawsons?"

Rebecca's voice lowered, and she quietly answered slowly. Levi did not notice, but she was now choosing her words deliberately. "Eight years ago, at the end of January 1841, Elizabeth gave birth to Malissa, her eighth child with Jacob. But I was no longer comfortable visiting regularly or willing to spend the night there. I helped Elizabeth when she gave birth to Malissa, but I told her it was time for me to move on and make my own way."

"What did you do then?" Levi asked.

Rebecca answered, "I went back to Papa Dawson and told him I'd like to do more work for him to save money for my own house. He seemed to like my company and happily agreed. He fixed up the room where I slept at the back of his house so it was a proper bedroom. It was a good arrangement, and I felt safe and happy."

"Did you ever go back to see Mr. Cook and Miss Elizabeth?"

Rebecca said, "Yes. Sometimes. We've both been over there, even just last summer."

Levi responded, "I remember Miss Elizabeth was nice, but Mr. Cook seemed like a grump."

"Ha!" Rebecca exclaimed, with a note of sarcasm she knew Levi would not detect, "I hadn't noticed."

Rebecca continued, "One day in May 1841, Papa Dawson noticed that my belly was getting larger and politely asked me if I was going to have a baby. He knew I wasn't married and that people didn't like to talk about an unmarried woman having a baby. But Papa Dawson was so calm. He looked at me with sincere concern. I told him I was several months along and expected it would be October before I gave birth.

"After that, Papa Dawson was very kind to me. He never asked who the father was. He only said, 'Rebecca, you've taken very good care of my children and me for some time and have never had a cross word to say. Now it's time for me to take care of you.' Then he told me that I shouldn't go into town anymore, that one of his sons would do the shopping until my baby, until YOU, came. Because they owned so many acres, Papa Dawson and his older sons were well known in Wayne Township. Papa Dawson's wife had passed away two years earlier, and he seemed unconcerned about what anyone thought of him."

Levi interjected, "I like this story. What happened then?"

"In September," Rebecca continued, "Papa Dawson called a midwife to examine me. She said I was doing well with my first baby and didn't expect any problems but to call her when the baby began coming. A month later, on October 11, 1841, you came into this world and changed my life forever. Each day, I found I could stand up for more extended periods, so I was soon able to prepare meals and manage the rest of the house. One day, when you were still only one month old, Papa Dawson knocked on the open door to my room where I was feeding you and asked if he could enter. I nodded that he could, and he came in with a gentle smile. He said:

'Rebecca, I told you back in May that it was my time to take care of you, and so now I am going to. I want to move you out of this small room and into the house's main bedroom if you agree to be my wife.'"

Rebecca paused before continuing. "I was surprised he asked, but I'd come to respect him as a sincere and responsible family man, so I agreed. Besides, I had no place else to go. One of our neighbors, Alan Gillmore, was a Justice of the Peace. He lived only a mile or two away. Papa Dawson sent word to Mr. Gillmore that he should come to our house on November 18, 1841, to perform a wedding. Mr. Gillmore showed up, thinking Papa Dawson would be marrying off one of his sons. But he stopped inside the doorway after arriving when his intended role became clear. He could see he was being asked to marry Papa Dawson and me – and I was holding my one-month-old baby. A few of Papa Dawson's sons and their wives were waiting to give their consent, so Mr. Gillmore got on with it, married us, and filed the marriage record with the County a week later. From that day until today, I was Rebecca Dawson. But you are, and will always be, Levi Ingledue, and Papa Dawson wasn't the least bit ashamed, nor would he put up with it if anyone dared to say a thing about it."

"You must have loved Papa Dawson very much," Levi said with youthful simplicity.

Rebecca dodged, "I came to love him. When he asked me to marry him, I knew he was a sincere and good man asking for permission to take care of you and me. I'd never been treated so kindly and couldn't help but feel affection. At first, it seemed like a simple trade. He was getting older and continued to need my help around the house. In exchange, I'd live in a stable setting where you and I could safely live and grow.

"After a few years," Rebecca said, "we realized we loved each other. Shortly after that, I gave birth to your brother AC. You were not even three years old when AC was born, so that you won't remember that, but you may remember when Milton was born two years later."

"Yes," Levi said, "I remember that and how happy Papa Dawson was. I like playing with AC and Milton."

"And now I'm about to have another baby, maybe a little sister," she said, "but it has gotten very late, and we must be getting home, or Papa Dawson will worry."

CHAPTER 8:
MEETING
JUDITH PARROTT

A sudden series of squeals of delight jolted Levi back to his 80th birthday party at the Krouskop's. Children were chasing each other around the yard inside the fence behind him. He turned around to take it all in and smiled. He realized that many of those happy children were here with their parents, some of whom were his children, and he concluded he was looking at his living legacy. But he knew that none of it would have happened without his beloved wife, Judith Emily Parrott, who had tragically died after a fire in their home in 1898, almost 25 years earlier.[50] He missed her greatly, but his

---

50   The family story is that the fire started from an oil-burning stove. It seems there ought to have been at least one newspaper article reporting this event; however, this author has not found any such articles.

memories of her were filled with the happy times of their life together. Levi smiled as he recalled her beauty. He turned back to the field and was instantly transported back in time to a farm that was only four miles southeast of where he was now standing. He remembered the day he first set eyes on the woman who became the love of his life.

"Levi!" Phillip Copeland shouted, "could you go down to the cellar, fetch that big bushel of apples, and put them by the table out here?"

It was the annual harvest celebration day for the Copelands in October 1860. The United States Census taker had visited in August, and Levi had been so proud to identify himself in his own right. Levi had worked as a farmhand for Phillip Copeland for almost a year. He was happy to finally find a place to live and call his own, even if it was only a shed behind the main house on the Copeland farm three miles southeast of Westminster, in Auglaize Township in Allen County, Ohio.

Levi did as Phillip asked and carried the heavy bushel of apples out of the basement. It weighed about 50 pounds but that was much lighter than the bags of seed and grain he often handled. As he emerged from the cellar, closed the doors, and headed across the lawn to the table, the morning sunlight spread across the farm past the big oak tree in the Copeland's yard.

There stood a girl, the rays of the sun behind her and the oak tree making her appear angelic. Levi stopped in his tracks and studied her. He was far enough away for her not to notice him watching her as he carried the apples to the big table that would be the hub of activity for that afternoon's party. He set the bushel down on the table, turned, and quickly went to find Phillip.

"Phillip," Levi said when he found him out in the barn, "who's that girl in the yard by the oak tree?" gesturing with his hand in the general direction.

"What girl?" Phillip asked.

"THAT girl," Levi said, again discreetly pointing directly to where the girl was still standing, gazing into the field.

"Oh, that's my cousin, Judith," Phillip said with a hint of amusement. "She lives with her father near Washington Court House, down in Union Township in Fayette County. Why do you ask?"

"She's ... uh ... beautiful," Levi answered haltingly.

"Would you like to meet her?" Phillip asked.

"Yes, I would, but she's dressed for the party, and I've only these work clothes," Levi said.

"That doesn't matter," Phillip said. "She's a farm girl used to hard work and has brothers used to the same. She won't pay any attention to what you're wearing."

Phillip had just turned 35 years old, was married, and had five children. He gently pushed Levi ahead of him out the barn door, and they began walking towards the oak tree. As they got closer, Phillip called out, "Judith! I've someone I'd like to introduce you to." Judith turned toward them, and it was then that Levi could see how beautiful she was.

"Judith, this is Levi Ingledue. He's been working with my boys and me on the farm for the past year. He's been a real help."

Judith studied Levi for a few seconds. Then she extended her right hand and said, "I'm pleased to meet you, Levi."

With that, Phillip felt he had done his job and turned around and walked away, leaving Levi in stunned silence. Eventually, Levi managed to reply, "And I'm also pleased to meet you."

Now, 61 years later, looking into the fields on his 80th birthday, Levi could not recall the rest of the words spoken between them that day, but the overwhelming emotion he felt in that moment stayed with him for the rest of his life. Judith had completely enchanted him.

Thus began a slow courtship lasting two years until they married.

About a year after they met, when they got the idea they might marry, Levi and Judith went for a walk near the Copeland farm for a picnic lunch. They stopped under an apple tree, just as Levi had done with his mother 12 years earlier. Levi began, "Judith, I think if we're going to be together much longer, you deserve to know more about me. I should tell you all I know now, so there will be no secrets or wondering between us."

He began by enthusiastically telling her the details of his Mama's stories about his family, where the Ingledues came from, and how he fit in. But then he turned to Judith and said, "Three months after my Mama told me all those stories, she died. She died just a week after giving birth to my sister, Mary. But Mary wasn't very healthy and, with Mama gone, Mary only lived a few weeks after Mama passed."

Judith felt a sudden wave of sadness even as she saw the sorrow on Levi's face when he told her of his tragedy. He saw her expression and assumed it reflected her empathy for his experience. He said, "I didn't mean to upset you. My mother died over ten years ago, and we don't need to talk about it."

She reached out, gently held his hand, and said, "Don't worry about it. I've had sadness in my life, but this is your story, and I want to hear the rest."

"After Mama and Mary died," Levi said, "Papa Dawson arranged to have both buried in a new cemetery a couple of miles north of Waynesfield (Horn Cemetery, *see* Figure 18, page 79). It's about five miles away from here. They rest next to the family of Papa Dawson's son, also named Joseph Dawson. But Papa Dawson was an older man when Mama died. Mama had helped support him, but he seemed to get old very quickly after Mama died. Papa Dawson struggled to keep house and care for AC, Milton, and me. He knew he needed to find us new homes. Even though I was only eight years old, I was the oldest and the first to leave his home."

"Where did you go?" asked Judith.

"Papa Dawson knew another Justice of the Peace, Nathan Woodbury. Nathan was married to Phebe, but they had no children. They'd moved here from New Hampshire and owned a small farm a few miles east of Waynesfield. They were developing a larger farm a half mile south when I came to stay with Miss Phebe in November 1849. Mr. Woodbury was working to develop the new farm in July 1850 when the Census people came to the smaller farm where I was living alone with Miss Phebe.[51]

---

51   *See* 1850 Census for Wayne Township, Auglaize County, Ohio, 25 Jul 1850. The head of the first house on the Census page (the 89th house visited in the Township) is identified as 45-year-old Phebe Woodberry, born in Massachusetts, with the following line listing Levi [ditto – meaning assumed last name was Woodberry], eight years

"But Mr. Woodbury got sick in 1855 and died in March 1856," Levi said. "Since he'd promised Papa Dawson he would care for me, Mr. Woodbury arranged for the County to assign me a legal guardian until I was of age. He asked two farmers who lived nearby, David Myers and Alexander Hutchinson, if they would accept me as a ward of the County. Even though the County didn't make it official until November 1856, I started working on the Myers and Hutchinson farms in late 1855 when I was 14. Miss Phebe was sad without Mr. Woodbury and only lived three more years. Mr. Woodbury and Miss Phebe rest in Berry Cemetery about eight miles away in Wayne Township in Auglaize County. Just like I often visit where my Mama and Mary rest, I often travel out there to be with the Woodburys.

"Just about when Miss Phebe died, I met your cousin Phillip," Levi said. "I think he was just passing through town one day, but Mr. Myers already knew him. Phillip mentioned he needed help on this farm, seven miles north of Waynesfield. Mr. Myers knew he didn't need as much help as he used to, knew I was going to be 18 soon and said that I could take a job with Phillip any time I wanted. That's how I came to live and work for him."

---

old born in Ohio. It is important to note that no other documents before or after 1850 support the existence of any Levi Woodberry (or Woodbury), so the last name Woodberry implied for Levi likely reflects the Census worker's assumption that Phebe did not attempt to correct.

CHAPTER 9:
LEWIS RUE INGLEDUE
AND HIS SON MARTIN

"I don't know if I skipped over some of the family details my Mama told me," Levi continued telling Judith, "but William and Magdalen Ingledue had a son, Lewis Rue Ingledue, who was about five years older than my Mama. Lewis and his wife, Nancy Erwin, had at least seven children and slowly moved west from Columbiana County in Ohio to Marshall County in Iowa.[52] Most

---

52   The 1856 Iowa Census reflects the presence of Lewis, his wife Nancy, and three sons living in Marietta in Marshall County, Iowa. Lewis' older son, William Marshall "Black Bill" Ingledue, was also present with his family. However, the 1860 US Census reflected (on 10 Aug 1860) Lewis and Nancy and their two sons (Martin and John) as residents in the area of the Westminster Post Office, Auglaize Township, Allen County, Ohio. Thus, it seems clear that it was some time after 1860 before Lewis Ingledue was fully settled in Iowa.

of Lewis and Nancy's children are starting their own families. Their fifth-born child was Martin Ingledue. He was born in 1837, so he's about four years older than me."

Levi continued, "By 1855, Lewis Rue, Nancy, and their family had begun moving to Marshall County in Iowa. But it's over 700 miles to Marshall County, and that was a long trip from Columbiana County. Allen County, Ohio, where we are right now, is about one-third of the way."

"Lewis and Nancy moved back here for a short time with Martin and his younger brother, John, just about the same time I started working with your cousin Phillip," Levi continued.

"Where does Martin live?" Judith asked.

"Right now, he's living with his mother and father, Lewis, a carpenter, only a couple miles from here."

"Have you met him?"

"Yes," Levi said, "but we've both been so busy that we've not had time to talk much."

"Do you know how he's related to you?" Judith asked.

"Martin is the grandson of my great uncle William Ingledue, so that makes us second cousins."

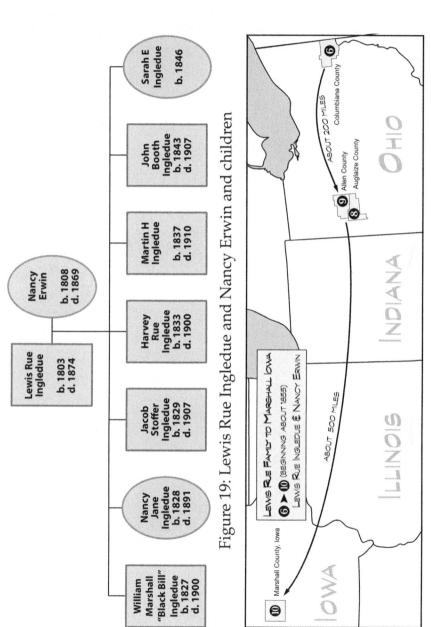

Figure 19: Lewis Rue Ingledue and Nancy Erwin and children

Figure 20: Lewis Rue Ingledue Migration to Marshall County, Iowa

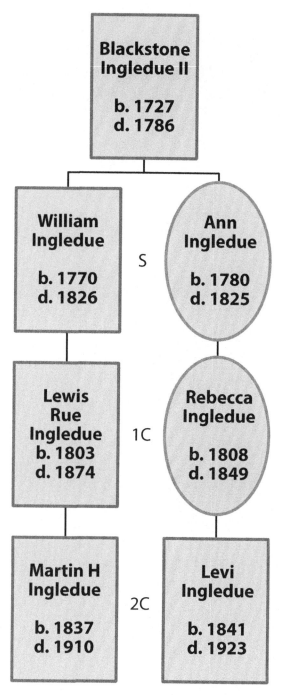

Figure 21: Lineage from Blackstone Ingledue II to
Martin Ingledue and Levi Ingledue

"But Martin knew your Mama, right?"

"Yes, I think he would have met her. Since it was such a long trip, Martin and his parents may have stayed with my Mama for a night or two as they traveled to and from Iowa."

"Do you think Martin knows who your father is?" Judith blurted out.

Levi was surprised by the sudden introduction of this challenging subject and backed away from Judith slightly.

Judith saw his reaction and quickly apologized, "I'm sorry. So sorry. I didn't mean to pry."

Levi thought about it for a few seconds and then did his best to answer, "I don't know if Martin knows, but I don't feel comfortable asking Martin about that right now. Maybe someday I can ask, but not now."

Levi's mind raced, searching for a polite way to change the subject without appearing to do so.

"You have listened to the story of my family for hours," Levi said, "but I just realized that I've not allowed you to get a word in to tell me the story of your own family!" Levi was excited to find such a worthy new topic.

CHAPTER 10:
JUDITH EMILY PARROTT'S HERITAGE

"You are correct! I've been selfishly listening to you share your family's story all this time," Judith said. "But, while I listened to your story, I reflected on the many parallels of your family's migration to that of my own."

Levi sat up, satisfied he had made a clean break, and said, "So tell me now!"

Judith began telling her story based on her family's oral history.[53] "My parents are John 'Blackbearded John' Parrott

---

[53] *The Parrett Migration*, by Dawn Parrett Thurston, is an excellent book that is arguably the most authoritative book on the subject of Parrotts/Parretts in the United States. Although there are independent records supporting the story Judith is about to tell, *The Parrett Migration* organizes most of the facts and details in such a comprehensive and authoritative manner that attempting to replicate it here would be improper. Anyone interested in the ancestry of the descendants of Levi Ingledue would do well to find a place in their library for this outstanding book.

and Mary Copeland, your employer Phillip's aunt. There have been so many 'John' Parrotts in my family that they all take on a nickname, so everyone will know who's who."

Levi smiled slightly at the inside joke he told himself, recalling the time he'd asked his mother if Blackstone Ingledew was a pirate. Judith saw the slight smile but did not associate it the way Levi had, so she continued.

"My grandfather was another John Parrott they called 'Smoking Johnny' Parrott. His father (my great-grandfather) was also John Parrott, but he didn't have a fancy extra name. Some people think his middle name was Preston. His father, my second great-grandfather, was Frederick Parrett, who had arrived from Europe spelling his last name with an 'e' rather than an 'o' as many of his descendants do."[54]

"Where did Frederick Parrett come from?" Levi asked.

"Europe. We don't know the exact details, but Frederick Parrett was from an area now mostly in Germany, along the long Rhine river that starts in the Swiss Alps, runs through Germany, and into the North Sea in Holland, now called The Netherlands. We believe Frederick – and perhaps his

---

[54] Variations in the spelling of "Parrott" are covered in substantial detail in *The Parrett Migration*. It is generally accepted that Frederick Parrett spelled his name with an "e." Still, there is ample record that his descendants used both Parrett and Parrott, sometimes due to changes by transcription becoming a matter of record. For example, Parrottsville in what is now Tennessee was settled by descendants of Frederick Parrett. In this book, "Parrott" is used in most cases since the dialogue presented is what someone would hear, not necessarily the spelling.

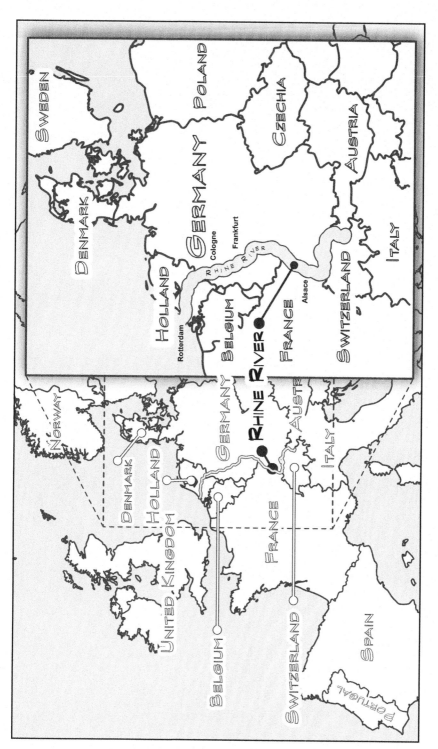

Figure 22: Origins of Frederick Parrett in Europe

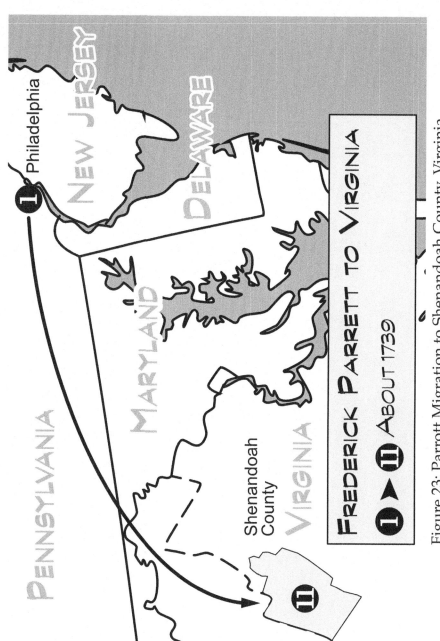

Figure 23: Parrott Migration to Shenandoah County, Virginia

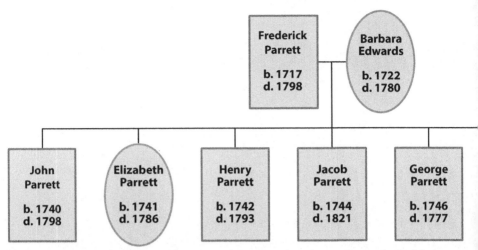

Figure 24: Frederick Parrett and Barbara Edwards and children

sister and other family members – sailed from Rotterdam in Holland to Philadelphia with countless others, mostly Germans, to arrive in Philadelphia around 1730."

Levi exclaimed, "1730? That's only five years after Blackstone Ingledew arrived in Philadelphia. Maybe they even met each other!"

"Perhaps." Judith smiled. "But Frederick would have remained close to other immigrants who spoke German and held similar religious views. We don't know where Frederick settled immediately after arriving in America, but there is some indication he found a home for some time near what is now Wilmington, Delaware. But in 1730, the Governor of Virginia was promoting farmland for sale in Virginia, so many Germans like Frederick began moving south into Virginia. In 1739, Frederick purchased 700 acres of land in Shenandoah County, Virginia.

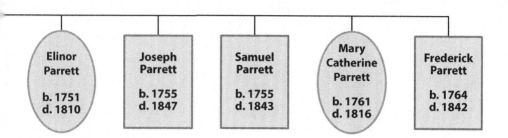

"By 1740, Frederick Parrett had moved near the village of Toms Brook, Shenandoah County. His wife Barbara had been born in Virginia and, there in Toms Brook, they began their large family of at least ten children."

"Golly, that's a big family!" Levi said. "It would be nice to have a big family where everyone could grow up with all those brothers and sisters."

Judith paused briefly to consider the implications of such a future with Levi. She smiled and continued, "Yes, most of their children and grandchildren grew up and had large families, creating many Parrotts. In 1740, Frederick and Barbara had their first child, John Preston Parrett, who was to become my great-grandfather."

Judith continued, "My great-grandfather John married my great-grandmother Catherina Meyers about 1761, and they

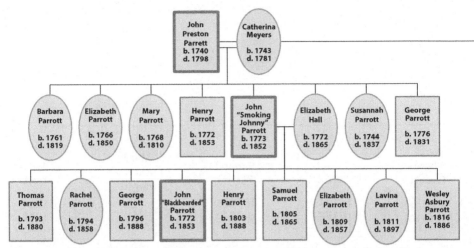

Figure 25 L: Two Generations of Descendants from John Preston Parrett and Catherina Meyers

began a family of their own just before the beginning of the American Revolutionary War. In 1777, at the age of 37, even with his growing family, great-grandfather John was the last of Frederick's seven sons to enlist in the militias to fight in the War. He only held the rank of Private in the militia during the War, but he served. Every Parrott man I have ever heard of has served in the military. Many of your ancestors were Quakers and were prohibited from engaging in military action. Still, Parrotts have a long history of military service and are proud of that service as part of their patriotic duty as a citizen.[55]

_____

55   Jacob Wilson Parrott, one of Judith Emily Parrot's third cousins, was born in 1843 in Fairfield County, Ohio, and subsequently enlisted in the Union Army during the Civil War. He later became quite famous due to his participation in a covert operation when he was only 18 years old in April 1862, just six months before Levi and Judith married. Jacob had volunteered to be part of what became known as the Mitchell Railroad Raiders. Parrott and his secret unit of Ohio infantry were dispatched deep into the Confederacy to steal a locomotive and destroy all the bridges and tracks, after crossing them, for over 100 miles of Georgia State Railroad tracks between Chattanooga,

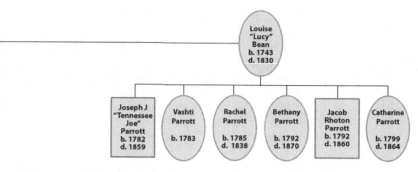

Figure 25 R: One Generation of Descendants from John Preston Parrett and Louise "Lucy" Bean

"Three of great-grandfather John's brothers, Samuel, Joseph, and Frederick Jr., personally witnessed the surrender of the British General Cornwallis in Yorktown on October 19th in 1781. Today, that surrender is widely understood to be the event marking the end of the War."

"That must have been wonderful to see!" Levi interjected.

Judith continued, "Great-grandfather John wasn't there at this historic event. In 1778, his wife, Catherina, became very ill just over a year after he'd enlisted. He was allowed to return home to care for Catherina and his small children. Soon after he returned, in about 1779, my great-grandmother Catherina passed away, having brought seven children into the world, the last in 1776, the same year the Declaration of Independence was signed. Great-grandfather John initially

---

Tennessee, and Atlanta, Georgia. Parrott and his unit were partially successful, but many were killed. Jacob was captured, tortured, and was one of the few to survive. He received the very first Congressional Medal of Honor. A museum is dedicated to him in his hometown, Kenton, Ohio.

relied upon help from the community to care for his children, but he remarried in 1781, this time to Louisa Bean. They called her Lucy.

"Lucy gave great-grandfather John *another* six children, the first of whom became known as 'Tennessee Joe Parrott.'" Judith explained that, "Soon after 'Tennessee' Joe Parrott was born, great-grandfather John and Lucy migrated 300 miles further southwest with all the younger children from Catherina. Great-grandfather John's sister, Mary Catherine, and her husband accompanied them to the western edge of North Carolina. Near his new homestead on Clear Creek, great-grandfather John formed the town of Parrottsville. Within ten years of arriving, the State of Tennessee took over Greene County, North Carolina, where Parrottsville existed. By 1797, Tennessee had renamed it Cocke County after one of its Senators. Many of my relations still live there today."

"They moved all the way down in Tennessee?" Levi asked.

"Yes," Judith answered. "It was a long way from Toms Brook, but it was a new frontier for a growing family. Around 1810, some more Parrotts – including my great grand-uncle, Joseph Parrott – who had previously moved from Toms Brook to nearby Rockingham County, Virginia, also moved to Parrottsville. Some of those Parrotts remained in Parrottsville for their entire lifetimes, but it wasn't long before others were again on the move.

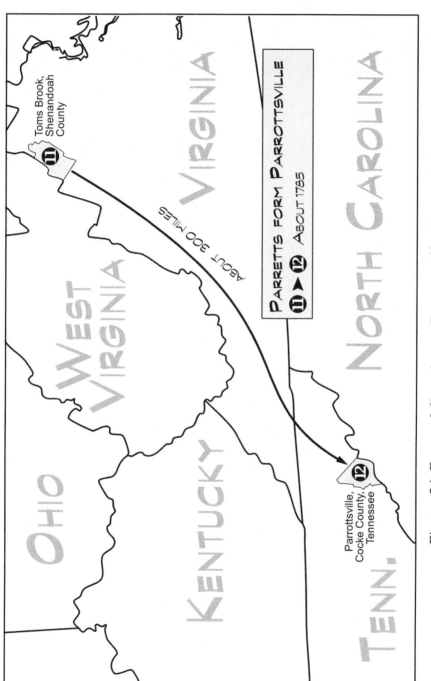

Figure 26: Parrott Migration to Parrottsville, Tennessee

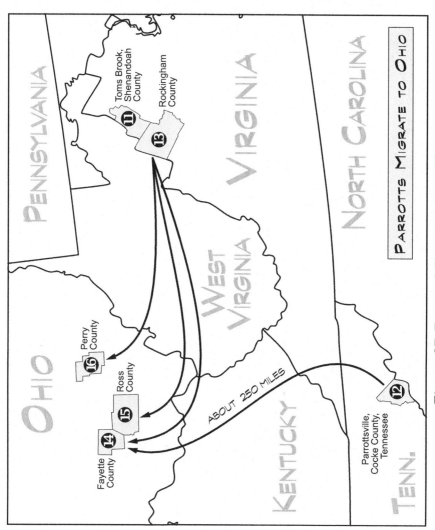

Figure 27: Parrott Migration into Ohio

"Less than 50 years ago," Judith continued, "in 1814, the Parrotts began looking to move northward. My grandfather, 'Smoking Johnny' Parrott, traveled 250 miles north with a large Parrott group from Parrottsville to resettle in Fayette County, Ohio, about 90 miles south of here. 'Tennessee Joe' and his family were also part of this resettlement from Tennessee. At about the same time, another group of Parrotts migrated west directly from Shenandoah and Rockingham Counties in Virginia to Fayette and Ross Counties in Ohio. Ross is next to Fayette County to the southeast. Some Virginia arrivals settled in Perry County about 30 miles southeast of Columbus, Ohio."[56]

"Were the Parrotts moving so much to find better opportunities?" Levi asked.

"Yes," Judith replied, "pioneer life in undeveloped areas is hard, but the Parrotts learned to thrive during a period of great migration for the family – even great migration for the entire country. My family has become financially successful by moving to an area, clearing and improving the land into farms, and looking for new opportunities."

Judith continued, "My father was born in 1800 in Parrottsville before moving to Ohio. They called him 'Blackbearded John' Parrott to distinguish him from his father, 'Smoking Johnny.' By 1820, my father was 20 years old and was living with his father in Fayette County, working on

---

56   See Appendix C in *The Parrett Migration*, by Dawn Parrett Thurston, for a list of the different Parrott family migrations to Ohio.

various farms. By 1850, just a few years ago, my father and his father, Smoking Johnny, had established a large farm in Union Township in Fayette County, with some 400 acres of land, a dozen horses, a dozen cows for milk, and many crops. My parents were married by Abner Copeland, my uncle, in 1825 in Greene County, Ohio, and then began having their eight children. I was the last of their children. I was born on March 22, 1843, on the family farm outside Washington Courthouse in Union Township in Fayette County and have been living there ever since."

Judith paused, a sad expression on her face held long enough that Levi asked, "Oh, Judith, what has upset you so?"

Judith replied, "Do you remember how sad I became when you told me your mother died when you were only eight?"

"Yes," Levi answered, "but why does that make you sad now?"

Judith replied, "My Mama also died when I was very young, just a week before my eighth birthday, in March 1850."

"Oh my goodness," Levi answered, "now I understand. You were not just feeling bad for me, but hearing of my Mama's passing reminded you that you'd lost your Mama at the same age as me. Did your father remarry?"

Judith said, "My father was sorrowful when my Mama died, and he remarried two years later to Rachel Whitcomb.

She was also a widow with several children from her first husband, but only one boy survived. That boy, John Stephenson Whitcomb, grew up and just married my sister Elizabeth! My father and stepmother, Rachel, support each other well, and now they have a five-year-old son, my little brother Samuel."[57]

---

57   John "Blackbearded John" Parrott married again on 9 Jun 1852, to Rachel Kirkpatrick Stephenson. Rachel had been married to John Turner Whitcomb until he died in 1841, leaving one surviving son.

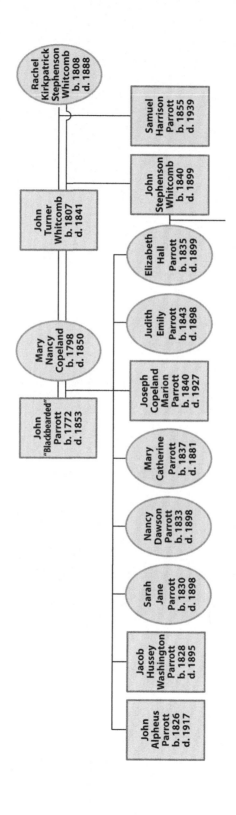

Figure 28: "Blackbearded John" Parrott children with Mary Nancy Copeland and
Rachel Kirkpatrick Stevenson Whitcomb

CHAPTER 11:
THE WEDDING OF LEVI INGLEDUE AND JUDITH EMILY PARROTT

"Pa!" Sadie Krouskop shouted out to Levi from the porch. "Are you feeling well?"

The sudden exclamation from his daughter interrupted Levi's memories that had been freely flowing while he had been gazing into the fields. He turned, looked at Sadie, raised his hand, and held it up, motioning that he was fine, fearing that his voice would not carry to the porch. He turned fully to see everyone still enjoying themselves on one of the last warm days of the year. He let out a short sigh. He realized all these people were here on this earth because of his Mama and his beloved Judith.

Not a day went by when he did not take a moment to reflect upon his life with Judith, but it was days like this that he felt both sad and celebratory. He knew that he and Judith had thrived with such a large and prosperous family full of love. He wished Judith could have been there to see all the fuss. But Judith had been killed in a horrible fire in their home over 20 years earlier, on July 18, 1898. He reflected on that for a few moments, smiling and waving to people who caught his gaze, then turned back to look out into the field.

On Thursday, October 13, 1862, two years after they first met, Levi Ingledue and Judith Emily Parrott were married at the First Presbyterian Church of Washington Court House in Union Township in Fayette County. One of the first members of this church was one of Judith's relatives. "Paintin' Joe" Parrott had joined the church in 1814 after arriving directly from Toms Brook in Shenandoah, Virginia.[58]

---

58   *Selected Histories of Fayette County Churches*, Maria Wilburn, 2003, page 26, cites Joseph Parrott, Sr., as joining the church in 1814.

Figure 29: Judith Emily Parrott and Levi Ingledue on their wedding day, 30 Oct 1862

Figure 30: "Blackbearded John" Parrott and
Rachel Kirkpatrick Stevenson Whitcomb, 30 Oct 1862

Twelve years before Judith and Levi's wedding, Judith's mother, Mary, had died, but her father, Blackbearded John Parrott, was present to give Judith away. Judith's stepmother, Rachel, was also present, as were all the Copelands. Martin Ingledue came down from Allen County. The only other nearby Ingledue who Levi had known was Elizabeth Ingledue. She was married to Jacob Cook and they had lived near Wapakoneta, but she had passed away just three weeks before the wedding, so no one else from Levi's family attended the ceremony.[59]

The wedding itself was presided over by the Reverend Samuel Miller, after which the parties gathered at the Parrott estate nearby for the reception. It was a brisk day on October 13, 1862, so most people stayed inside, sipped warmed apple cider, and enjoyed meeting family and friends. About an hour after the party began, Martin Ingledue walked up behind Levi, placed his hand on his shoulder, and quietly said, "Levi, if you have a moment, I'd like to talk to you privately, perhaps on the front porch."

Levi turned and saw Martin's serious expression. Levi followed Martin out the front door onto the porch, quietly closing the door behind them. Martin looked carefully

---

59   The presence of Martin Ingledue at Levi's wedding is perhaps likely. Still, here it is conjecture to imagine that it was Martin who learned who Levi's father was, and then gave this information to Levi.

around to make sure they were genuinely alone before he began speaking.[60]

"Do you remember last year when you asked me if I knew who your father was?"

"Yes," Levi said. "Have you learned something?"

"I have," Martin said solemnly, "and now I know why your mother was so careful and didn't want to tell you until you were older and would understand."

"Do you think I can finally be told?" Levi asked.

"I think so," Martin said, "but it might help you to understand how I came to learn what I know. When you asked about this last year, I sensed it might be a sensitive subject in our town, so I proceeded quietly with discretion. The first person I visited was your stepfather, Joseph Dawson. He was 80 years old when we spoke last month. My experience is that, when people get that old, they become less concerned about 'secrets' and what others might think, so I hoped he might have some ideas he would share with me. We had a good conversation. I don't believe he knew with certainty who your father was, but he was adamant that he wasn't your father."

---

60   This conversation is a fictional account of what almost certainly happened at some point. Rebecca Ingledue would not have told her 8-year-old son who his father was and his father was unlikely to come forth on his own.

Levi said, "Well, I knew that much."

"Even so," Martin continued, "Joseph told me about when your mother became his wife just a month after you were born. He said that she'd been working for a few years as a domestic helper in his home in Waynesfield but also performed similar duties in the home of her cousin Elizabeth Ingledue, my aunt, out near Wapakoneta. Back then, Elizabeth Ingledue was married to Jacob Cook. Joseph told me that, in 1839, your mother Rebecca bought a home lot on the east end of a new town, Uniopolis, on the road between Wapakoneta and Waynesfield. Even though she hadn't yet married, Joseph thought she intended to build a house and settle there. But Joseph said that your mother came to him in early 1841, asking if she could do more to help in Joseph's home. Your mother said she thought Joseph might need more help since his wife had died just over a year earlier, and he still had children in the home that needed care. Joseph told your mother it was true he needed help, so she moved into a back room and began working for him full-time."

Levi said, "Yes, my Mama told me about that."

Martin continued, "Joseph told me that he sometimes wondered why Rebecca would stop working for her kin like that, especially after he noticed she was going to have a baby. Shortly before you were born, Joseph told Rebecca that he would marry her after you were born and protect her, but that he wanted to know who your father was, without any judgment, and promised to keep it a secret.

"One night, in September 1841, before you were born," Martin continued, "your mother confided to Joseph that Jacob Cook was your father. She knew that was a serious problem because Jacob was already married to her cousin – my aunt – Elizabeth Ingledue. Joseph was an honorable man and has kept your mother's secret all these years. I think he only told me because he's gotten so old that it didn't seem as important as it used to be. I also think he may have figured out I could have been asking on your behalf and knew I'd tell you because, at this point, you had a right to know, and you're now old enough to be careful with the knowledge."

Levi said, "I remember Jacob Cook and Elizabeth too. I remember Jacob Cook being gruff sometimes. I guess maybe now I know why."

Martin said, "Despite your Papa Dawson's opinions, I wanted to talk to Jacob Cook about the matter. My aunt Elizabeth died just a few weeks ago, so I recently rode over to Wapakoneta to visit Jacob to pay my respects to him and his family. When I was there, I directly asked Jacob what he knew about who your father was. After some uncomfortable fidgeting, he admitted he was your father. He said that since both Rebecca and her cousin Elizabeth were no longer with us, he didn't think anyone was around who could be hurt much if you knew. Still, he thought, and I agreed, that it wasn't a good topic for public conversation."

"Did he say how it came to be that he had a baby with my Mama?" Levi asked.

136

"No," Martin said, "he didn't say, and I didn't ask because it seemed clear he wasn't comfortable talking about any of it in the first place. He also didn't seem interested in hearing from you about it. So I'd leave that alone."

"So that's it?"

"Yep," Martin said, "but I'd think long and hard before you ever tell anyone."

Levi said, "I have to tell Judith. She's now my wife. We've already discussed this, and I think she deserves to know the truth."

"Fair enough," Martin said. "Let's go inside before we attract any attention."

A few days later, Judith asked Levi what he and Martin had been whispering about on the porch after their wedding. Levi carefully recounted his conversation with Martin, including the conclusion that this was not information to be made public. Judith quickly agreed. Levi and Judith never again spoke with each other about it, but at least some of their adult children learned of Levi's origins, and they discreetly passed the knowledge down.[61]

---

61   See the story attributed to one of Levi's granddaughters, Helen Frances Ingledue Hover, in the section *About Levi Ingledue's Origin* within Roy D. Ingledue's *The Family Ingledue* manuscript excerpted in Appendix A at Page 10 within this book.

CHAPTER 12:
LEVI'S
GROWING FAMILY

Shortly after they were married, Judith's father made good on his promise of a dowry, giving them enough money to go out on their own. Five years after they were married, on July 31, 1867, Judith paid $2,800 for 140 acres of land east of New Hampshire in Allen County, Ohio. But she sold it two years later, in August 1869. By that time, Levi was following an Ingledue family tradition and was engaged in clearing and improving land for farming. So it seems a better deal than improving the New Hampshire property may have come along.

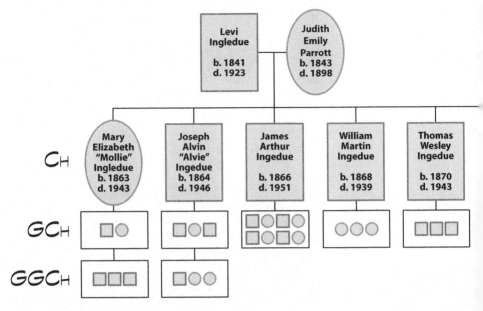

While his business was growing, so was Levi's family. Over 23 years, Levi and Judith had 11 children, all of whom grew to adulthood, and all had children of their own. By his 80th birthday, Levi already had 30 grandchildren and six great-grandchildren.

Levi and his family frequently moved around in western Ohio in search of arable land they could work on, whether they owned or leased it. During this period, many owners of forested properties leased their land to industrious pioneers like Levi. Levi, and others like him, would bring men and machines to clear the land of trees, build fences around it, harvest and sell the rest of the lumber, and then return the new farm to the owner (see Figures 32 and 33).

LEVI INGLEDUE'S DESCENDANTS
AS OF HIS 80TH BIRTHDAY
ON OCTOBER 11, 1921

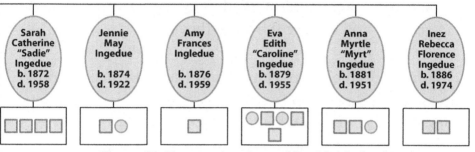

Figure 31: Four generations of Levi Ingledue's
descendants as of his 80th birthday

Figure 32: Levi Ingledue and his crew with Ox-drawn
D. June Steam Engine, ca. 1883

Pictured on the preceding page (Figure 32) is an illustration based upon a photo of Levi atop an ox-drawn Champion[62] steam engine typically used to power a sawmill (not shown), whip in hand. Levi and his crew used the sawmill to create lumber from the trees on land they had cleared. In the background, you can see the fence they built.

Sadie Ingledue's sons, Lloyd and Ralph Krouskop, often lamented the day when Levi "retired" and came to live with them. In 1917, Levi released the last parcel of land he and Judith had owned together and moved into George and Sadie Krouskop's home; one they had bought in 1912 to house their growing family. Lloyd told his son that, as a child, he and his brother, Ralph, (aged 10 and 13 when Levi arrived) resented the fact that Levi was treated with such honor and deference. Levi took their room in the house and always got the best cuts of meat for dinner!

Lloyd provided to Roy D. Ingledue the photograph in Figure 33 with an expanded caption for inclusion in Roy's 1981 unpublished manuscript, *The Family Ingledue:*

"Levi sitting on the flywheel of a D. June Traction Engine which he acquired later. The driver's seat and the steering wheel

---

62   Champion was the brand name of a steam engine patented in 1875 by D. June & Co., Fremont, Ohio. The company was established as June & Curtis in 1853, becoming June & June by 1856 and, by 1859, D. June & Co. The company built the Champion portable steam engine in the 1870s and the Champion steam traction engines (1875–1905), self-contained girder frame engines with subbase, stationary steam engines and boilers of any size, from 10hp to 150hp, Champion pony saw-mills, and Locomotive boilers for oil wells.
See: http://vintagemachinery.org/mfgindex/detail.aspx?id=2197

Figure 33: Levi Ingledue and Daughter Amy with D. June Traction Engine, ca. 1889

Figure 34: The children of Levi Ingledue, ca. 1898

can be seen just ahead of the left rear wheel. (I'm sure Ralph Nader wouldn't approve this arrangement). The steam line seen running from the engine (to the right) is thought to be supplying steam to a small canning plant. The Buzz-saw positioned in front of the engine was used to supply fuel for the boiler. It is uncertain who the girl sitting atop the saw is, but it is believed she may have been one of Levi's younger daughters. These pictures were probably made during the 1870s." - Roy D. Ingledue [63]

The children of Levi Ingledue, ca. 1898 (Figure 34, preceding page): The handwritten caption on the back of the photo on the preceding page, presumably written by Lloyd Krouskop, said, *"Ingledue Children of Levi & Judith Emily (Parrott) Ingledue."* From left to right, they are arranged by age, youngest at left, oldest at right, with common name and birth year shown:

Florence (1886), Myrtle (1881), Caroline (1879), Amy (1876), Jennie (1874), Sadie (1872), Tommy (1870), Willie (1868), Arthur (1866), Alvie (1864), and Mollie (1863).

---

63   The photograph in Figure 33 was almost certainly not taken during the 1870s. In 1875, Levi would have been 34 years old. In this photo, Levi's beard has a substantial amount of gray hair (but still some black), suggesting he may be no younger than 50 years old. Assuming the girl on the table saw is one of Levi's daughters, a review of the possibilities based on their ages is essential. The girl on the table saw appears to be 10–15 years old. The birth years of Levi's daughters are Mary "Mollie" (1863), Sarah "Sadie" (1872), Jessie (1874), Amy (1876), Eva (1879), Anna "Myrtle" (1881), and Inez "Florence" (1886). The facial structure of the girl is not consistent with Mary's. Photo enhancement creates an image most comparable to other photographs of Amy. Amy would have been 12 years old in 1888, so it seems this photo is likely to be of Levi and Amy and was taken between 1886 and 1891.

Given that Inez Rebecca Florence (furthest left in Figure 34), was the youngest and was born June 14, 1886) and appears to be approximately 12 years old, this photo would have been taken about 1898, the same year Judith Emily Parrott was killed in the fire.

One of Levi's great-grandsons, Jerald "Jerry" Smeck, lent an excellent copy of a studio photo on the facing page (Figure 35). It depicts Levi with his children, a photo that many Ingledues have seen. Some even have it framed in their homes. Florence is seated in the front row, right of Levi. Florence seems about five years older than the precdeding "1898" photo (Figure 34), so this photo was probably taken about 1903. The names of each person are included below, as is the first name often used by the family. Also included are the years of their birth and death. Married names are included in parentheses.

Given Levi's apparent age in the photo (about 62 years old) and the fact that Judith is not in the portrait, it seems likely this photo was taken after her passing in 1898.

Back Row: Joseph Alvin Ingledue "Alvie" (1864–1946); James Arthur Ingledue "Arthur" (1866–1951); Jennie May (Stout) "Jennie" (1874–1922); Eva Edith (Cole) "Eva" (1879–1955); Amy Frances (Berry/Keipper) "Amy" (1876–1959); William Martin Ingledue "Willie" (1868–1939); Thomas Wesley Ingledue "Tommy" (1870–1943).

Front Row (continued on page 153)

Figure 35: Levi and his children, ca. 1903

Figure 36: Levi and his daughters, 1912

Figure 35 Front Row *(continued from page 148)*: Anna Myrtle (Patterson) "Myrtle" (1881–1951); Mary Elizabeth (Butters) "Mollie" (1863–1943); Levi Ingledue (1841–1923); Inez Rebecca Florence (Coulter) "Florence" (1886–1974); Sarah Catherine (Krouskop) "Sadie" (1872–1958).

Levi would have been about 71 years old in the 1912 photo on page 151 (Figure 36). His hairline has receded, and his beard is all white (compared to full hair and darker beard in the studio photo (Figure 35) estimated to be from 1903). Additionally, each daughter is visibly older than in the studio photo. The inscription on the back identifies the daughters, left to right, as being *(full name and life span added by this author)*:

- "Florence": Inez Rebecca Florence (Coulter) (1886–1974)
- "Mert": Anna Myrtle (Patterson) (1881–1951)
- "Eva": Eva Edith (Cole) (1879–1955)
- "Amy": Amy Frances (Berry/Keipper) (1876–1959)
- "Jen": Jennie May (Stout) (1874–1922)
- "Sadie": Sarah Catherine (Krouskop) (1872–1958)
- "Mollie:" Mary Elizabeth (Butters) (1863–1943)

CHAPTER 13:
CONCLUSION

As stated at the beginning of this book, the purpose of this research was to establish and prove the parents of Levi Ingledue. It does not comprehensively describe all Ingledue descendants in America from the 1700s. Still, to verify the conclusions herein, it was necessary to exhaust all available research options to develop a tree that left no other alternative than what the evidence universally (and exclusively) supports. Although some other theories existed in family lore, no evidence exists that is inconsistent with the conclusion that Jacob Cook and Rebecca Ingledue were Levi's parents.

Still, several additional topics are covered in four appendicies that follow:

A. An overview of previous Ingledue genealogy work (limited to the Ingledues in the United States), and

B. Discussion of the DNA technology, data, and analysis forming the basis of the conclusions, and

C. Areas requiring further study, and

D. The historical and current prevalence of Ingledews in Yorkshire, England.

APPENDIX A: PREVIOUS INGLEDUE GENEALOGY

ALICE LEE INGLEDUE

In the late 1970s, the second wife of Elwood Martin Henry Ingledue,[1] Alice Lee *Smith* Ingledue, undertook a large-scale effort to find every Ingledue in the United States and document their relationships. The scale of that effort is remarkable, especially given that Alice Lee was not a genealogist and there was no such thing as the Internet, much less Ancestry.com™.

Although her conclusions may not satisfy modern genealogical proof standards, Alice Lee established a vast network of "cousins" as part of a good-faith effort to construct a massive Ingledue family tree. Alice Lee's method was to write letters to and correspond with everyone named Ingledue found in the phone books her husband collected on his hotel business trips. Some of the details were not always accurate, and she admits to not knowing the connection for some branches of people with whom she corresponded, but the gigantic sheets of sections of the Ingledue family tree that remain are, to this day, remarkable reference tools.

In October 1980, Alice Lee produced and distributed many copies of an otherwise unpublished 107-page "book" along with huge poster-size trees and individual family stories. Through at least 1989, Alice Lee continued to receive correspondence

---

1   Blackstone Ingledew > Blackstone Ingledue II > William Ingledue > Lewis Rue Ingledue > Martin H. Ingledue > Charles Wilson Ingledue> Elwood Ingledue

and send updates to her network of "cousins." Jerald "Jerry" Smeck[2] was kind enough to send me the best copies he had of Alice Lee's book and other materials she had gathered and distributed. Those documents have been faithfully scanned and are available here:

https://www.ingledue.net/ AliceLeeIngledueDocs/

ROY DARWIN INGLEDUE

In January 1981, one of Levi Ingledue's grandsons, Roy Darwin Ingledue,[3] distributed a 69-page manuscript of his own, *The Family Ingledue*, almost all of it crediting Alice Lee Ingledue's work and correspondence. Roy's manuscript discussed the mysterious origins of his grandfather Levi Ingledue and had a series of pages containing family tree segments. Perhaps because it was based at least in part on Alice Lee's prior work, Roy's manuscript contains several errors and unsubstantiated conclusions (including incorrect identification of Levi's mother as a 13-year-old girl, Nancy Jane Ingledue). Still, it is clear Roy sought to advance and share the collective knowledge of the Ingledue family

2   Levi Ingledue & Judith Emily Parrott > Eva Edith (Caroline) Ingledue & Lindon Albert Cole > Florence I Cole & George Washington Smeck > Jerald "Jerry" Smeck

3   Levi Ingledue & Judith Emily Parrott > Thomas Wesley Ingledue & Libbie Blound Estry > Roy Darwin Ingledue

Roy's January 10, 1981 manuscript and tree charts have been scanned and are available here:

https://www.ingledue.net/TheFamilyIngledue/

Roy included a section in his manuscript titled, *About Levi Ingledue's Origin.* Within this section, Roy had several quotes from letters written to Alice Lee Ingledue in which various theories were advanced, primarily by Levi's descendants, regarding Levi's heritage. Some of these are entirely speculative. Some are pretty entertaining. Others are what one would call examples of "family lore" that may have at least some factual basis. Thus, when examining these stories, every effort has been made to treat each of them as "true" until presented with facts showing they could not be accurate. The section from Roy's manuscript, *About Levi Ingledue's Origin,* is transcribed in the next few pages with a few corrections for spelling/grammar. Several footnotes have been inserted in this section of Roy's manuscript to document the ancestry of the individual making the comments (or being discussed).

Of all the theories advanced, the theories advanced by Helen Frances Ingledue Hover (see Appendix A, Page 10), one of Levi's granddaughters, have since been discovered to be well-supported by DNA science.

ABOUT LEVI INGLEDUE'S ORIGIN
Roy D. Ingledue

Although he became the patriarch of a sizable
branch of the Ingledue family that became all
that completely separated from the main lineage,
none of his living descendants can recall ever
hearing of who his real mother was, or where she
belonged in the order of descent.

Half a dozen relatives contacted recall having
heard a rumor that his birth was "illegitimate,"
that his mother's name was Elizabeth, and that
she was married to a man named Cook. It was
assumed by many that she was his mother.

Since the genealogy charts now reveal (as never
before) the actual dates in the sequence of
events, it becomes obvious that Elizabeth would
not have been his real mother, since she was
already married in 1823 to Cook (Levi was born in
1841). She would have been 38 years old at the
time and his name would have been Cook instead
of Ingledue. Elizabeth was the sister of Lewis
Ingledue[4] who had 6 children.

Lewis's 6 children are listed here, 2 of which
are daughters, and a son, Martin H. Ingledue. In
a recent letter from Mrs. Raymond Haas, formerly
Audrey Ingledue[5] (Levi's granddaughter), she

---

4   Blackstone Ingledue II & Ann Rue > William Ingledue &
Magdalen Erwin > Lewis Rue Ingledue.

5   Levi Ingledue & Judith Emily Parrott > James A. Ingledue &
Edna M. Brosey (adopted name) > Audrey M. Ingledue.

A-4

quotes her Aunt Florence (Coulter)[6] as saying "I think his mother was one of uncle Mart's sisters."

Martin had 2 sisters, Sarah who was yet unborn in 1841, and Nancy Jane who was about 13 at that time. It seems very plausible that she [Nancy Jane] was Levi's real mother, a fact that he himself may never have known. By her aunt Elizabeth taking him to raise, the very young Nancy Jane was spared the stigma of being an unwed mother.

If these deductions are indeed correct as believed, then the rightful connection has been established between Levi and the main branch of the family and the two branches are united again, thus solving many mysteries about our relationship.

---

6   Inez Rebecca Florence Ingledue was Levi's daughter and wife of George Edwin Coulter. She died on 11 May 1974.

RANDOM EXCERPTS

Taken from letters from contributors, sent to
Mrs. Elwood (Alice Lee) Ingledue, in response to
her letters of inquiry while compiling data on
the Genealogy of the Ingledue Family.

From Lloyd G. Krouskop:[7]

My Grandfather Levi lived with my folks for
many years after the death of his wife. He
was the only Grandfather I ever knew, as my
Grandfather Krouskop died before I was born.
I used to go to his room and ask him about
his family when I was small, but I never got
anywhere. He would tell me that he was hatched
out on a stump in the woods, and that was the
end of it.

I talked with my cousin, Helen (Ingledue)
Hover[8] of Findlay, Ohio, who is a daughter of
William Martin Ingledue, son of Levi Ingledue.
She told me that her mother, Mary (Stuber)
Ingledue[9] told her that, while visiting
William's sister Mary (Mollie Ingledue)
Butters,[10] they were looking at old photographs
and they saw a picture that they couldn't figure

7   Levi Ingledue & Judith Emily Parrott > Sarah "Sadie" Ingledue
& George S. Krouskop > Lloyd George Krouskop.

8   Levi Ingledue & Judith Emily Parrott > William M. Ingledue &
Mary Stuber > Helen Frances Ingledue.

9   Mary Lillian Stuber was the wife of Levi's son William Martin
Ingledue.

10   Mary Elizabeth "Mollie" Ingledue was Levi's daughter, and
wife of Joseph A. Butters.

out. They asked Mollie about it and she said, "Oh, that's that old COOK who was Pa's father." Helen's sister Ruth[11] had told me of that also, so I think he may have been Levi's stepfather.

From Mildred (Ingledue) Sandy.[12]

My Aunt Florence Coulter[13] told me, just a year or two before she passed away, that Levi was an illegitimate child, and since then one of my cousins told me that his mother, a daughter of Levi, had said that too. I wonder if he may have been raised by his Grandparents and took their name?

---

11   Ruth Marie Ingledue was a daughter of William Martin Ingledue and Mary Lillian Stuber, and a wife to James T. Meek.

12   Levi Ingledue & Judith Emily Parrott > James A. Ingledue & Edna M. Brosey (adopted name) > Mildred E. Ingledue.

13   Inez Rebecca Florence Ingledue was Levi's daughter and wife of George Edwin Coulter. She died on 11 May 1974.

From Dr. Grace (Ingledue) Barnhart:[14]

> I note in Roy's[15] letter to you, he mentions
> that Levi (his and my Grandfather) had his
> mother's last name. I recall as a small child,
> asking kid questions of him, and one answer
> was, "I don't know – ah – you see, I was a
> woods colt." My next question was, "What's
> that?" Answer: "Wh – er – I was illegitimate."
> By that time, I guess I either sensed that
> I was asking questions kids weren't supposed
> to ask grown-ups, or else I simply became
> disinterested. The information must have been
> correct since it came from Levi himself.

From Grace Wolf Ingledue (Mrs. Walter):[16]

> I had not heard the expression "Woods Colt."
> Just talked to a friend and she said that she
> had – that [it] indicated two young people had
> gone for a trot into the woods.

---

14   Levi Ingledue & Judith Emily Parrott > William Martin
Ingledue & Mary Stuber > Grace Emaline Ingledue.

15   Levi Ingledue & Judith Emily Parrott > Thomas Wesley
Ingledue & Libbie Blound Estry > Roy Darwin Ingledue.

16   Blackstone Ingledew > Blackstone Ingledue II > Blackstone
Ingledue III > Reason S. Ingledue > James Ingledue > George E.
Ingledue > Walter James Ingledue married Grace Wolf on 25 Dec 1932.

From Mrs. George W. Smeck:[17]

A friend of mine, who is a writer for our newspaper, knew of the expression "Woods Colt." She said it meant the person was illegitimate.

From James O. Wilhelm:[18]

Elizabeth bore one child out-of-wedlock, soon after which she married Joseph Cook (Mormon records say Jacob Cook). Levi could not have been this child, since she was married in 1813 and Levi's birth was in 1841.

---

17   Levi Ingledue & Judith Emily Parrott > Eva Edith (Caroline) Ingledue & Lindon Albert Cole > Florence I Cole.

18   Blackstone Ingledue II & Ann Rue > William Ingledue & Magdalen Erwin > James L. Ingledue & Sarah Davis > Sarah Jane Ingledue & Solomon T. Wilhelm > James Owen "J.O." Wilhelm.

From Mrs. Helen (Ingledue) Hover:[19]

Grandpa Levi was an illegitimate child, raised by an Ingledue family, so we assume his mother was an Ingledue girl and her parents raised him. We think his mother later married a Dawson, as Grandpa had a half-brother, A.C. Dawson.

If one reads all this carefully, it seems that the identity of Levi's father was a known – but closely guarded – fact amongst his children, even if it was never openly discussed. It is unclear how they came to know that "Old Cook" (Jacob Cook) was Levi's father, but the information most likely came from Levi himself or possibly Judith Emily Parrott.

Linden Krouskop contributed the photo at right (Figure 37) of Alvin C. "AC" Dawson, Levi's half-brother, taken around 1885 in Lima, Ohio, at a photography studio owned by E. T. Bowdle. AC and his brother Milton had relocated to be raised by other Dawsons in Iowa after their father's death in 1864. They returned frequently to their roots in Allen County, Ohio, and were known to the Ingledues. Levi's children and grandchildren all apparently called Levi "Pa" so the handwriting on the back could be anyone in the family.

19   Levi Ingledue & Judith Emily Parrott > William M. Ingledue & Mary Stuber > Helen Frances Ingledue.

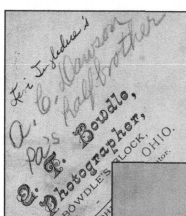

Figure 37: A.C. Dawson, ca. 1885

APPENDIX B:
DNA ANALYSIS

Because it is probably exceedingly dull to all but the most patient readers, this book will not detail the extensive DNA-related research and analysis used to help decode Levi's ancestry. Using autosomal (AncestryDNA™) and YDNA (FamilyTreeDNA™) tests of samples contributed by dozens of Ingledue descendants and others, an extensive database has been amassed and cross-referenced with other research to reach several conclusions with an <u>extremely high</u> degree of confidence:

Levi Ingledue's mother was Rebecca Ingledue. A record exists for the marriage of Joseph Dawson and Rebecca Ingledue on November 18, 1841, just a month after Levi was born on October 11, 1841. Rebecca subsequently had three children with Joseph, one of whom was Alvin "AC" Dawson, who Levi's children understood to be Levi's half-brother. The third child, Mary, was born on June 28, 1849, but there were apparently complications from childbirth, and Rebecca, then 41 years old, died three weeks later on July 19, 1849. Baby Mary died three weeks after that, on August 8, 1849. Both Rebecca and Mary rest next to each other and other Dawsons in the middle of Horn Cemetery, north of Waynesfield, Ohio (See Figure 17, page 79).

Rebecca Ingledue was a descendant of Blackstone Ingledue. Thus, Levi Ingledue was not just an Ingledue by name only. Customized analysis of AncestryDNA™ match data proves it. By cross-referencing AncestryDNA™ matches for dozens of descendants of seven different children of Levi Ingledue and Judith Emily Parrott, a persistent pattern emerged: Descendants of Levi Ingledue matched with 16 <u>other</u> AncestryDNA™ tests from descendants of Blackstone Ingledue who did not descend from Levi. These 16 matches descended from two sons of Blackstone Ingledue II (1727–1786) and Ann Rue: William Ingledue (1770–1820) and Blackstone Ingledue III (1775–1846). Collectively, these 16 matches also all had multiple matches to Levi's descendants in a manner that cannot be coincidental.

Levi Ingledue's father was Jacob Cook, who was already married to a pregnant Elizabeth Ingledue (Rebecca's first cousin) when Levi was born. In addition to AncestryDNA™ (suitable for identifying relatively close common ancestors of autosomal DNA matches), three people also submitted samples for YDNA testing. YDNA tests can definitively identify paternal lineage and are therefore limited to male donors, but the reliability is extremely high.

In this case, where family lore suggested that Jacob Cook was Levi's father, three men provided samples of both AncestryDNA™ and YDNA testing to explore the theory:

a. Jay Cook is one of Jacob Cook's third great-grandsons.[20] It was beneficial that Jay Cook was a descendant of Jacob Cook's <u>second</u> wife, Margaret Jane Metcalf. The fact that Jay Cook descended from Margaret Jane Metcalf (not Elizabeth Ingledue) ensured that any matches of Jay Cook to the "Levi group" could only be due to matching DNA from Jacob Cook and not to DNA from Elizabeth Ingledue, Jacob's first wife.

b. Christopher Ingledue is one of Blackstone Ingledue's seventh great-grandsons but is <u>not</u> a descendant of Levi Ingledue.[21]

c. William Ingledue is one of Levi Ingledue's great-grandsons.[22]

---

20 Jacob Cook & Margaret Jane Metcalf >
   John Elmer Cook & Laura Ann Smith >
     Lewis Jacob Cook & Cora E. Wilson >
       Warren George Cook & Mary Alice Carney >
        Warren Eugene Cook >
         Jay (Jacob) Cook

21 Blackstone Ingledew & Elizabeth Palmer >
   Blackstone Ingledue II & Anne Rue >
     William Ingledue & Magdalen Erwin >
       Lewis Rue Ingledue & Nancy Erwin >
        William Marshall 'Black Bill' Ingledue & Phebe Jane King >
         William Lloyd Ingledue & Mary E. Monroe >
          William Isaac Ingledue & Augusta Warner >
           Glen Louis Ingledue & Margaret Ruth Thomas >
            Timothy Lynn Ingledue & Linda Synder >
             Christopher Ingledue

22 Levi Ingledue & Judith Emily Parrott >
   James Arthur Ingledue & Edna Mae Brosey >
     Harry Thomas Ingledue & Lucille Frances Lones >
       William Michael Ingledue.

The results of the AncestryDNA™ and YDNA testing of these three men were as follows:

a. Jay Cook was a strong YDNA match to William Ingledue (67 markers in the R-M269 Haplogroup) but not Christopher Ingledue. Jay did not have an autosomal AncestryDNA™ match with William Ingledue, but Jay did have an AncestryDNA™ match with William's sister, Judy. Also, Jay did not match AncestryDNA™ with any of the tested "Blackstone only" matches. This is compelling evidence that Jacob Cook was Levi's father since no other circumstance could account for these matches.

b. Christopher Ingledue and William Ingledue did not have a YNDA match. Christopher's closest matches all had the surname MacAulay which has apparent origins in North Uist, an island and community in the Outer Hebrides off the west coast of Scotland.[23] This location is conspicuous because other records indicate most Ingledews came from the east coast of England, but many Ingledews were masters and mariners, so who knows?

A higher-definition "Big Y" analysis of this YDNA test has been completed and is currently being evaluated to try identify when a "MacAulay" became an "Ingledew." However, this probably occurred before surnames were widely used by commoners.

---

23   Figure 3, a map of the United Kingdom on page 17 of this book, shows where North Uist is.

In any case, this YDNA result proves modern-day Christopher Ingledue and William Ingledue did <u>not</u> have a common <u>paternal</u> ancestor.

However, because Levi's children carried DNA from Rebecca Ingledue, Christopher Ingledue <u>did</u> have a number of AncestryDNA™ matches with other descendants of Levi Ingledue, matches that reflect them all as descendants of Blackstone Ingledue.

On the next page, there is a "screen shot" showing the participants and key matches in the "Levi Ingledue DNA Research Project" (Figure 38). It is unlikely to be legible in this book, but you can view a larger version here:

https://www.ingledue.net/DNA/

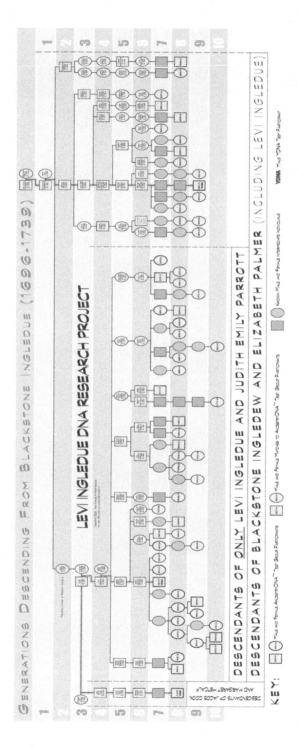

Figure 38: DNA Test Group and Matches

APPENDIX C:
AREAS REQUIRING
FURTHER STUDY

Having solved the paternal and maternal heritage of Levi Ingledue, a number of questions remain and bear further research. The following subjects are beyond the scope of this work but would likely provide some additional reference points for the Ingledue family on both sides of the Atlantic. Some work is done. Much more to do.

Identifying Rebecca Ingledue's Mother: This author's identification of Ann Ingledue as Rebecca Ingledue's mother is a theory with some circumstantial support but without proof sufficient to meet modern genealogical proof standards. Although there is solid evidence of shared DNA between Levi's descendants from separate children of his and several descendants of Blackstone Ingledue (people who are not descendants of Levi), there seems to be no "proof" as to who Rebecca Ingledue's parents were. Analysis of all Ingledue families of the time shows that no Ingledue men could have fathered Rebecca (and kept it out of Quaker and civil records). Further, there were no other Ingledue women of the right age and unmarried such that they could have given birth to Rebecca Ingledue and allowed Rebecca to keep that surname. This book characterizes Rebecca Ingledue's mother as Ann Ingledue because Ann is the only mother that fits without conflicting facts.

Identifying Rebecca Ingledue's Father: This author was unable to identify any potential fathers for Rebecca Ingledue.

One idea was that Ann Ingledue's "master," William Hatcher, had impregnated Ann, but searching for DNA matches with Hatchers in their trees did not yield any relevant results.

<u>Why Was Blackstone I Only Bequeathed Six Shillings?</u> The discrepancy between the inheritance given by father, William Ingledew, to his son Blackstone compared to the estate he bestowed upon Blackstone's half-brother Caleb and full-sister Elizabeth is conspicuous. Why did they get so much, and he got so little?

<u>Did Anyone "Consent" to Blackstone I's Marriage?</u> There is "family lore" that an "Aunt Elizabeth Smith" gave consent within the Quaker community in England for Blackstone Ingledew to marry Margaret Pattison (Patterson) because both Blackstone's parents had died. However, this author has not found any such relative or Quaker document describing such consent (although Meeting records document their allowance of the marriage to go forward). As this book goes to press, the Durham Record Office in England remains closed for rennovation. They are reportedly imaging old records including Quaker Meeting Records. A research trip is contemplated in 2024.

<u>Who Was William Ingledew's Father?</u> Was Blackstone's father, William Ingledew, the brother of Leonard Ingledew with common roots in Newby near Seamer-in-Cleveland?

<u>Whatever Happened to Caleb Ingledew?</u> Caleb Ingledew, William Ingledew's first son and Blackstone's half-brother, inherited the family homestead in Newby. If any male(s) known to be continuous paternal descendants of this Caleb Ingledew can be identified, a YDNA test could establish common paternal ancestry of Ingledew descendants on both sides of the Atlantic. An "adult" baptism record from

1698 for Caleb Ingledew was found in Guisborough, North Riding, Yorkshire, but no further records were found. Caleb Ingledew was also found listed in a 1705 will for William Ingledew of Newby (but this is obviously not the will for his father who died in 1698).

Where is the Will of Elizabeth Ingledew? Besides being curious whatever became of Caleb's sister Elizabeth, the will of Blackstone's sister, "Elizabeth Ingledew," who died in England in 1746 and left an estate of considerable value to benefit Blackstone's children in America has not been located. Similarly, no documentation shows the specific amount of the inheritance Blackstone Ingledew's children received. Elizabeth was Blackstone Ingledew's sister. Their father had bequeathed to Elizabeth substantial interests in his business, including ships, which were to be held for her benefit until she reached majority or married. It is also not known if "Elizabeth Ingledew" ever married before she died, but a will would probably clear up much of this if her will can be found.

As this book is going to press, a thorough examination of records in the UK has been completed by a professional genealogist to help discover details with respect to at least to the last four items above.

APPENDIX D:

HISTORIC AND CURRENT PREVALENCE OF
INGLEDEWS IN
YORKSHIRE

The precise relationship between William Ingledew, father of Blackstone, and other Ingledews in northeast England has not been established. However, a review of available birth, marriage, and death (BMD) indexes reveals the existence of a cluster of at least four dozen Ingledews living in Seamer-in-Cleveland during the 1650s to 1720s, an area abutting William's presumed family estate in Newby. It is implausible that these Ingledew families were all unrelated to William, but the specific relationship is unknown. If one or more well-documented living male descendants of these Ingledews could be identified, YDNA tests would help establish the relationship of modern Ingledews in England to modern Ingledues in America.

In America, Ingledue (or Ingledew) is an uncommon surname, a fact that has aided the reconstruction of the family tree of Blackstone Ingledew descendants in the United States. In the United Kingdom, however, the surname Ingledew is more common. Though there are records of Ingledews all over the United Kingdom today, the area of old County York remains a "hot spot."

A search on the UK version of Findmypast resulted in 1,649 records with "Ingledew" (or similar) in records all over the UK prior to 1750. Almost 65% used the Ingledew spelling and another 13.5% used Ingledue. The remaining 21.8% of the records used other variations, differences resulting from either transcription errors, literacy of the scribe, or local custom.

SURNAME	COUNT	PCT
INGLEDEW	1066	64.6%
INGLEDUE	223	13.5%
INGLEDOW	186	11.3%
ENGELDEW	68	4.1%
INGELDEW	54	3.3%
ENGLEDUE	23	1.4%
ENGELDOW	14	0.8%
INGELDUE	11	0.7%
YNGLEDEW	2	0.1%
ENGELDUE	2	0.1%
YNGELDEW	–	
YNGELDOW	–	
YNGELDUE	–	
YNGLEDOW	–	
YNGLEDUE	–	
TOTAL	1649	100%

The prevalence of Ingledews in Yorkshire was implied in a popular series of books from author James Herriot.

In Chapter 1 of *All Things Bright and Beautiful* (the second in the series of books by Yorkshire veterinarian James Herriot beginning with *All Creatures Great and Small*), a story is told of a late-night visit to Harold Ingledew near Therby village who had a ewe in trouble but was very intoxicated when Herriot arrived. While there is no such place as "Therby," there is a

Thirlby, a small village on the edge of the North York Moors national park about five miles east of Thirsk (Thirsk was the real-life location for much of Herriot's veterinary practice). The second episode of the second season of the original televised series on BBC1, *All Creatures Great and Small*, titled "Attendant Problems" first aired on September 23, 1978. In this episode, the "Harold Ingledew incident" is portrayed much as described in the book, except that it depicts Siegfried Farnon visiting Mr. Ingledew. In 1997, researcher and author Michael J. Rossi wrote *James Herriot, A Critical Companion*. He included character sketches and analysis from the books, including that of Harold Ingledew, describing him as a "small, quiet man in his seventies."[24]

In 2020, a new televised series of *All Creatures Great and Small* was introduced on Channel 5 in the United Kingdom. As of the date of this publication, three seasons of the new series have aired but there is no portrayal of the visit to Harold Ingledew's farm to see a ewe in trouble. However, a man referred to only as "Mr. Ingledew" appears at the veterinary practice in Season 2, Episode 3, titled "Semper Progrediens." It is implied that Mr. Ingledew lives near town because he is returning one of the hens that had escaped the makeshift chicken pen at the back of the practice and found her way to his farm. Later in the episode, Mr. Ingledew returns with a basket of eggs laid by the escaped hens. They decided to give Mr. Ingledew all the chickens.

It seems certain that the author of *All Creatures Great and Small* (James Wight, writing as James Herriot) did not use Harold Ingledew's real first name in the book. Still, there were still dozens of Ingledew households in Yorkshire, North Riding, as late as 1940 when the events in *All Creatures*

---

24   *James Herriot: A Critical Companion*, Appendix B, page 178. The author does not cite a source for the stated age or stature of this Harold Ingledew.

Great and Small transpired. It is also a fact that Thirsk (called Darrowby in the *All Creatures* books) is about 20 miles south of Newby, near Stokesley, the apparent family estate of William Ingledew (father to Blackstone Ingledew who emigrated to America in 1725).

While the relationships of these 1940 Yorkshire Ingledews to Blackstone Ingledew is not presently known, the uniqueness of the name and the geographic proximity strongly suggests these Yorkshire Ingledews share a common ancestry with Blackstone Ingledew.

BIBLIOGRAPHY

Although many resources were used in researching the details recited in this book, it is impossible to list them all. Still, in aid of future research, here are *some* of the books and publications used and cited within this book.

Books and Publications:

Allen, Frank M., ed. *History of Fayette County, Ohio.* Indianapolis: B. F. Bowen & Company, Inc., 1881.

Bell, Carol Willsey. *Columbiana County Ohio, Marriages 1800–1870.* Youngstown, Ohio: Bell Books, 1990.

Bell, Carol Willsey. *Columbiana County, Ohio, Newspaper Abstracts Volume 1.* Youngstown, Ohio: Bell Books, 1986.

Bell, Carol Willsey. *Columbiana County, Ohio, Newspaper Abstracts Volume 2.* Bowie, Maryland: Heritage Books, 1987.

Bell, Carol Willsey, ed. *Columbiana County, Ohio & Vicinity Bible Records Volume 1,* Youngstown, Ohio: Bell Books, 1986.

Bell, J. P., Co. *Historical Sketch of Bedford County, Virginia, 1753–1907.* Lynchburg, Virginia: J. P. Bell Co., Inc. 1907.

Boyd, Gregory A. *Family Maps of Allen County, Ohio.* Norman, Oklahoma: Arphax Publishing Co., 2009.

Boyd, Gregory A. *Family Maps of Auglaize County, Ohio.* Norman, Oklahoma: Arphax Publishing Co., 2006.

Duncan, Patricia B. *Index to Loudoun County, Virginia, Personal Property Tax Lists*. Westminster, Maryland: Willow Bend Books, 2004.

Evans, Lyle S., ed. *A Standard History of Ross County, Ohio – Volume II*. Chicago and New York: The Lewis Publishing Company, 1917.

Fry, Joshua, and Peter Jefferson. *A map of the most inhabited part of Virginia containing the whole province of Maryland with part of Pensilvania, New Jersey and North Carolina – 1751*. London: Thomas Jefferys, 1755.

Grose, Polly. *Hannah: The Story of Hannah Ingledew Janney 1725–1818*. London: William Sessions Limited, 1997.

Hay, Donna. Quakers in Great Britain – 1650s–1750s. 2013. Retrieved January 5, 2023, from https://haygenealogy.com/hay/quaker/quaker-GB.html

Herriot, James. *All Creatures Great and Small*. New York: St. Martin's Press, 1972.

Herriot, James. *All Things Bright and Beautiful*. New York: St. Martin's Press, 1974.

Hiatt, Marty, and Craig Roberts Scott, ed. *Loudoun County Virginia Tithables 1758–1786 Volume 1: [1749], 1758–1769, 2d Ed.* Athens, Georgia: Iberian Publishing Company, 2011.

Hinshaw, William Wade. *Encyclopedia of American Quaker Genealogy, Volumes 1–7*. 1936 et. seq.

Hopkins, Margaret Lail, ed. *Index to The Tithables of Loudoun County, Virginia and to Slaveholders and Slaves - 1758-1786,* Baltimore: Genealogical Publishing Co., Inc., 1991.

Hutchison, Louisa Skinner. *Apprentices, Poor Children, and Bastards, Loudoun County, Virginia 1757-1850.* Westminster, Maryland: Heritage Books, 2008.

Hutchison, Louisa Skinner. *Index to Loudoun County, Virginia, Wills 1757-1850.* Westminster, Maryland: Heritage Books, 2012.

Ingledue, Alice Lee Smith. *"Ingledue".* Unpublished. 1980.

Ingledue, Roy Darwin. *The Family Ingledue.* Unpub., 1981.

Jeffery, Nesta. *Index to the Columbiana County Ohio Marriage Records 1803-1833.* Lisbon, Ohio: Nesta Jeffery, 1989.

Jeffery, Nesta. *Index to the Columbiana County Ohio Marriage Records 1833-1848.* Lisbon, Ohio: Nesta Jeffery, 1990.

Mack, Horace. *History of Columbiana County: Illustrations and Biographical Sketches: Some of its prominent men and pioneers.* Philadelphia: D.W. Ensign & Co., 1879.

McCarty, De Wayne C. *Newspaper Abstracts from the Villages of Columbiana and East Lewistown, Ohio.* Apollo, Pennsylvania: Closson Press, 2008.

McClellan, C. A. O. *Map of Auglaize County, Ohio.* Newton, Connecticut: C.S. Warner, 1860.

McCracken, George E. *Penn's Colony, Volume 2 - Welcome Claimants.* Westminster, Maryland: Heritage Books, 2007.

McMurray, William J., ed. *History of Auglaize County Ohio – Volume I.* Indianapolis: Historical Publishing Company, 1923.

Meyers, Albert Cook. *Quaker Arrivals in Philadelphia, 1682–1750.* Philadelphia: Ferris & Leach, 1902.

Miller, Charles C., ed. *History of Allen County, Ohio and Representative Citizens.* Chicago: Richmond & Arnold, 1906.

Newland, Samuel J. *The Pennsylvania Militia: Defending the Commonwealth and the Nation, 1669–1870.* Annville, Pennsylvania: Commonwealth of Pennsylvania, 2002.

Roberts, Helen E. *Researching Yorkshire Quaker History: A Guide to Sources.* Kingston upon Hull, East Riding, Yorkshire, England: University of Hull – Brynmor Jones Library, 2003 (rev. 2007).

Rossi, Michael J. *James Herriot: A Critical Companion.* Westport, Connecticut: Greenwood Publishing Group, 1997.

Shepherd, Walter Lee, Jr. *Passengers and Ships Prior to 1684 – Volume 1 of Penn's Colony.* Westminster, Maryland: Heritage Books, 2006.

Thurston, Dawn Parrett. *The Parrett Migration.* Memoir Mentor Books, 2014.

Unger, Jane. *The Ships of Penn's Fleet.* West Chester, Pennsylvania: Chester County Pennsylvania Genealogy Project, 2011. Retrieved January 6, 2023, from https://www.chester.pa-roots.com/misc/ships_of_penn.htm

Wilburn, Maria. Selected Histories of Fayette County Churches. Washington Court House, Ohio: Carnegie Public Library, 2003. Retrieved January 15, 2023, from https://www.cplwcho.org/sites/default/files/attachments YETTE%2520COUNTY%2520CHURCH%2520HISTORIES.pdf/

Additional Resources:

D. June & Co., Fremont, OH, U.S.A. Tifton, Georgia: VintageMachinery.org, 2014. Retrieved January 7, 2023, from http://vintagemachinery.org/mfgindex/detail.aspx?id=2197

Map of Europe. 2023. Retrieved from World Vectors by Vecteezy, https://www.vecteezy.com/free-vector/world

Quaker Meeting Records (various) from County Durham, Yorkshire, and Northumberland, United Kingdom, 1650–1800.

<u>Library and Related Resources</u>:

Auglaize County Recorder and Probate Offices, Wapakoneta, Ohio

Boone County Historical Society, Lebanon, Indiana

Bowling Green State University – Center for Archival Collections, Bowling Green, Ohio

Durham County Record Office, Durham, United Kingdom

Durham University Library Archives and Special Collections, Durham, United Kingdom

Earlham University, Richmond, Indiana

Lima Public Library, Lima, Ohio

The National Archives, London, England, United Kingdom

North Yorkshire County Council Archive, Yorkshire, United Kingdom

Presbyterian Historical Society, Philadelphia

Salem Public Library, Salem, Ohio

Thomas Balch Library, Leesburg, Virginia

William & Mary Libraries – Special Collections Research Center, Williamsburg, Virginia

<u>Online Services</u>:

Ancestry.com™ (a registered trademark of Ancestry.com Operations Inc.)

AncestryDNA™ (a registered trademark of Ancestry.com Operations Inc.)

FamilySearch™ (a registered trademark of Intellectual Reserve, Inc.)

FamilyTreeDNA™ (a registered trademark of Genealogy by Genetics, Ltd.)

Findmypast.uk (a trademark of Findmypast Ltd, London)

GEDmatch™ (a registered trademark of GEDmatch, Inc.)

newspapers.com (no longer a registered trademark)

ACKNOWLEDGEMENTS

The author would like to thank the following people for their help with this project. Some of these people are no longer with us, but they deserve recognition. The use of alphabetical order does not reflect an assessment of the value of their help.

Jeanne Albright

Robyn Ballerini

Barbara Brookin

Betty Bryant

Jeff Cole

Jan Comiskey

Roxanna Conner (Evans)

Jacob W. "Jay" Cook

Carol Cox

Cara Jones

Elizabeth Mae Crist

Melissa Cutlip

Don Dawson

Steven Dow

Mary Engledow-Walton

Jean Estry

Ginger Ferguson

Polly Grose

Gaynor Halliday

Martha Rebecca Hutchison

Alice Lee *Smith* Ingledue (1907–1996)

Chris Ingledue

Jim Ingledue

Karon Kay Ingledue

Karon Susan Ingledue

Roy Darwin Ingledue (1906–1994)

William Ingledue

Mary King

Sally Knight

Becky Knightly

Linden & Colleen Krouskop

Kristy K. McCoy

(continued)

Lynn McCuistion

Jenny McFarland

Jill McShane

Judy Newland

Julie Osborn

Suzannah Polivka

Samuel Polivka

Gabriel Polivka

Rachel Reddy

Emily Rorick

Frederick Skill

Jerald "Jerry" Smeck

Rocky L. Snow

Jan Thomas

George Turns

Jan Wilkes

Maxine Willett

David Wonder

Doreen Wortman

Edie Wright

ABOUT THE AUTHOR

Born on August 22, 1957, in Providence, Rhode Island, Mark Leslie Hunnibell is the second of four children of Kenneth Lee Hunnibell and Carol Linda Dutra. Both Kenneth and Linda had been students at the Rhode Island School of Design (RISD), as had many in Mark's extended family. Shortly after Mark was born, his father bought and moved the family to an old farm homestead (originally built in 1786) in Rehoboth, Massachusetts. When Mark was about six years old, his parents divorced and he moved with his mother and three sisters to a home in a subdivision about forty-five miles north of the old farm homestead. Six years later, they moved to Kensington, California—a small community just north of Berkeley.

Mark attended junior and senior high schools in Richmond, California, where he graduated in June 1975. Two months later, he returned to live with his father in Rehoboth while continuing the family legacy at RISD in Providence, Rhode Island. Although Mark frequently demonstrated his creative abilities in studies at RISD, he spent more time with extra-curricular activities and, when it came time for him to graduate in June 1979, he was nine credits short to receive his Bachelor of Fine Arts in Industrial Design. Intent on moving back to California, Mark drove across the country in the summer of 1979. He remedied his credit shortfall by taking a full semester of journalism and psychology classes at the University of California, Berkeley, and had the credits transferred back to RISD. After completing his coursework at Cal Berkeley, he worked as an automotive machinist in Albany, California.

In September 1980, finally motivated to put his RISD degree to use, Mark and Geoff, his friend from RISD, drove across the country from California to the east coast. Geoff was taking a new position in Washington, DC. Mark would live with his father in Rehoboth while he assembled his design portfolio to begin his career as a designer in New York. Mark and Geoff were on an extremely tight budget for the trip (they each started with $100), so they camped and stayed with friends along the way on their ten-day trip.

Back in Rehoboth one morning, after a long night working on his design portfolio, Mark announced to his father at breakfast that, rather than pursue a design career, he planned to join the Air Force to be a pilot. The announcement was so unexpected and the concept so preposterous that his father — always the practical man — insisted he immediately go into Providence to meet with the USAF recruiter to find out if anything Mark was talking about was possible. At dinner that evening, Mark reported that it was a real program and that he qualified for it with his RISD degree. His father asked what he was going to do. Mark replied, "Oh, it's done," explaining that he had already signed up and the first exams had already been scheduled.

Less than a year later, Mark made his solo flight in an Air Force T-41 — a Cessna 172 airplane the Air Force used to determine if a flight candidate had the skills to complete jet training. Mark passed this screening program and, in December 1981, received his commission as a 2nd lieutenant. In May 1983, after more than a year of intensive military pilot training, Mark arrived at his first assignment as a C-130 pilot at Clark Air Base in the Republic of the Philippines. In October 1985, he transferred to a WC-130 unit at Keesler Air Force Base in Mississippi, "the Hurricane Hunters." Mark completed his military service at the rank of Captain and was honorably discharged from the Air Force effective January 5, 1989.

In October 1988, just two months before Mark was scheduled to separate from the Air Force, he met Laura at Keesler Air Force Base. Laura was a registered nurse who had just joined the Air Force as a First Lieutenant. Four months later, Mark began what would become his twenty-nine-year career as a pilot for American Airlines. He and Laura married in New Orleans about two years after they first met.

Beginning during his time in the Philippines, Mark acquired substantial knowledge and expertise in computer programming and was a pioneer in using desktop computers to write and run custom applications to support operational Air Force missions. In 1986, he received an account on the Defense Data Network—one of the first applications of the TCP/IP communications protocol originally called ARPANET—a network now known as "the Internet."

While at American Airlines, Mark became active in the Allied Pilots Association, the labor union exclusively representing the pilots at American Airlines. He personally developed the union's first "members only" website and suite of services. In 1998, he was elected and served as a representative union officer for two years. From 1998-2009, he oversaw the professional Information Technology department within the union that administered the second and third generations of the Internet services he had brought forth.

In the mid-1990s, Mark began exploring his family history using a combination of ancestry.com and its offline-capable software package, Family Tree Maker. Over the years, his wife Laura saw how he could dive deep into genealogical issues, so she asked him to help solve her own family mystery, the subject of this book.

Made in the USA
Las Vegas, NV
27 May 2023

72612137R00132